The Complete
Guide to
Customer
Service

THE COMPLETE GUIDE TO CUSTOMER SERVICE

LINDA M. LASH

WILEY

John Wiley & Sons
New York   Chichester   Brisbane   Toronto   Singapore

Copyright © 1989 by John Wiley & Sons, Inc.

Library of Congress Cataloging in Publication Data:
Lash, Linda M.
    The complete guide to customer service/Linda M.
Lash.
        p.   cm. — (Wiley series in training and development)
    Bibliography: p.
    ISBN 0-471-62428-4   9-89 BT 22.00
    1. Customer service.   I. Title.   II. Series.
HF5415.5.L37 1989
658.8′ 12—dc19   88-14898
                                            CIP

Printed in the United States of America

10 9 8 7 6 5 4 3

For my mother,

who said I should always be nice to customers,
and Reinhard Kondelka, who is.

Preface

In 1969, I put on a "We try harder." button and began to serve customers at an Avis car rental desk in Syracuse, New York. I had no idea what I was doing, but I needed the money. The Avis manager in Syracuse at the time wasn't sure how long a university student would stay with Avis, so he didn't waste any money sending me away for training or buying me a uniform.

After a year, an Avis training roadshow came to my city, and I was allowed to attend a short training session about how to serve customers. It was a big day for me. I learned a lot, and I also met the director of training, Russ James, who later asked me to join the training department. He told the rest of his team that he had hired the world's worst rental sales agent, a sobriquet he devised after watching me serve customers.

I spent the next 15 years working with Avis people in the United States, Canada, Australia, Europe, Africa, and the Middle

East to deliver the caliber of car rental service our customers expect. The work also brought me into contact with other companies and organizations.

In 1985, I conducted a session on customer contact training at "Training '85," a training conference sponsored by *Training* magazine. I was surprised by the number of participants who chose to attend this session and the enthusiasm they showed. I took great pains to use many examples from companies other than Avis, and I tried very hard not to use the name Avis. But, halfway through the session, one of the participants—I'll call him the Hostile Heckler—decided to comment that he didn't see anything very great about Avis service, and he didn't know why he should be listening to an Avis person on the subject of service. He went on to relate a car rental experience with Avis where he used a number of tricks to pose as an employee of a certain company and receive a special rate for his Avis car rental. The only thing I could think of to say to Mr. Hostile Heckler was to ask him if he enjoyed the car. He said yes, and before he could say more, I said, "Good! It's time for the coffee break."

The point is that Avis does not give perfect service all of the time. Very few companies do. But Avis is a dynamic company that constantly tries new ideas—and even old ideas again—to improve service. Each day around the world, since 1962, thousands of Avis employees put on a "We try harder" button and try to live up to this famous advertising slogan. I'm one of them, and I hope I'll be one for a long time to come.

In my work at Avis and with other companies, I've heard a lot of good ideas from employees at all levels who care about the service they and their companies give. Some are just good ideas. Some are better than others. And some will make the company a lot of money. The most difficult task by far is making them work.

Like most other authors, I've had a lot of encouragement from friends, from colleagues at Avis, and from service establishments who receive my custom. Special thanks go to all of these people, as well as to Mike Hamilton, Charles Peers, Martin Broadwell,

Anne Bayton, Marc Grainer, Arlene Malech, Liz Winterhalter, Eric and Mary Ann Allison, Lesley Colyer, Alice Webb, and the 1988 winter season bar staff at the Hotel Klosterbraeu—Gerhard Huber, Reinhard Kondelka, Johannes Suntinger, and, my sweet inspiration, Juergen Spiss.

LINDA M. LASH

Bracknell, Berks., England
September 1988

Contents

The Complete Guide to Customer Service

1

The Bottom Line on Quality

In 1980, British Airways had a persistent record of lateness, slow baggage delivery, and indifferent service on board. Among European business travelers at the time, British Airways was known as the world's worst airline. Among British business travelers, British Airways meant flying the flag—and enduring it with a stiff upper lip. The airline was also unprofitable.

In 1985, British Airways was the Airline of the Year, winning the coveted award from *Executive Travel* magazine in a poll of its readers. In addition to winning the overall award as Airline of the Year, British Airways scored highest in two key areas: airline with the best overall cabin staff and airline with the best in-flight staff. At the same time, this change in service produced results on the bottom line, taking the airline from unprofitable and overstaffed to profitable, and headed for privatization.

What caused such a dramatic turnaround? Perhaps the newer and cleaner planes, the new image, and better food. Or that a far greater percentage of flights leave and arrive on time, and baggage delivery is better. Possibly the award-winning television commercials that support the change, the employees' new uniforms, and newspaper reports of internal management structure changes and staffing reorganizations. Or the addition of new routes and new services based on careful market research. "All of these strategies are important," says Sir Colin Marshall (the title was conferred following a highly successful public flotation), chief executive of British Airways, "but the element of customer service and Putting People First is the most crucial."

CUSTOMER SERVICE

Sir Colin Marshall uses two key words in this statement: customer service. They've become a standard part of our vocabulary. The *World Book Encyclopedia Dictionary* (1963) gives its first definition of customer as "a person who buys, particularly a regular patron of a store." A second definition is "a person one has to deal with." For service, this same dictionary gives a first definition as "a helpful act or acts; aid; conduct that is useful to others."

In fact, customer service has become a broad activity, encompassing all of the following:

- a department that receives telephone calls and letters from dissatisfied customers and answers them,
- a front-line service employee who is pleasant and helpful to customers,
- a repair engineer who arrives promptly and fixes a problem with a machine, computer, or device,
- a waiter or waitress who delivers the correct order of food promptly and pleasantly,
- a hospital out-patient clinic that efficiently and pleasantly moves patients in and out of the clinic,

- a government agency that promptly and pleasantly offers the advice needed by a taxpayer,

- a bank clerk who promptly and efficiently processes check reorders,

- a pharmaceutical sales person who promptly and pleasantly supplies pharmacies with the latest products and is able to provide accurate information about them,

- a car manufacturer that promptly and efficiently supplies its dealers with new cars and the right parts,

- a training department that effectively supplies its company or organization with training programs that solve performance problems,

- a switchboard that promptly and efficiently handles telephone calls,

- a telecommunications company that promptly and efficiently installs a telephone system,

- a construction company that builds new homes on schedule, or

- a steel mill that promptly delivers the right products to its buyers.

Our definition of customer service activities in recent years has broadened to encompass these activities and many more. For a long time, the words "customer service" were used only in the positive sense, meaning good customer service that was prompt, efficient, pleasant, helpful. In today's economy, the two words can be modified by an adjective. There's good customer service, and there's bad customer service.

A NEW CHOICE

With these adjectives in use, consumers have a new choice: to buy good or bad customer service, just as they can choose to buy a good apple or a bad apple, a good television set or a bad television set.

With consumer choice come the standard economic concepts of supply and demand and pricing. Consumers will now choose and pay for good service, just as they will choose and pay for a good apple or a good television set.

With these concepts of choice on the customer service side come the traditional roles of competitors, even in activities that have historically been monopolies. While consumers have in the past fought their way into city and town centers to get to a U.S. post office, they now give much of their business to shopping mall postal centers that happily mail parcels at a higher price.

Thomas J. Peters and Robert H. Waterman, Jr., in their best-selling book *In Search of Excellence,* identified eight basic principles or attributes they found to be characteristic of large companies having a history of profitability. One of these attributes they call "close to the customer." Their research indicates that these profitable companies "learn from the people they serve. They provide unparalleled quality, service, and reliability."

LINK TO PROFITABILITY

This chapter would be very short if the following syllogism could be accepted as fact:

- All companies and organizations that deliver superior customer service are very profitable.

- All companies and organizations that do not deliver superior service are not profitable.

- Therefore, to be very profitable, a company or organization must deliver superior customer service.

The reality is that both profitable and failing businesses deliver poor customer service. Even more surprising, both profitable and unprofitable businesses deliver *superior* customer service. Thus the relationship between profitability and customer service is not obvious.

MEASUREMENT OF SERVICE

Profitability can be determined by many concrete measurements, depending on a company's or organization's goals: return on equity, net profit margin compared with competitors, compound asset growth, compound equity growth, return on total capital, dividends, share of market growth, earnings per share, and so on.

Customer service does not have this range of concrete measurements. It may be easy for a group of people to agree on one or two top performers in a given field in terms of customer service. One example is Maytag, which features "ten years' trouble-free operation" and the idle Maytag repairman. One might compare Maytag with its competitors such as General Electric. The service ratings a consumer might give both companies relate to their own experiences, with the products of the two companies, with advertising they have seen, or based on word-of-mouth advertising from friends. But the consumer might have difficulty comparing Maytag's service with the service given by Neff or Miele, which market their products primarily in Europe.

To compare profitability, Maytag's net profit margin or return on equity can be compared with that of General Electric, Neff, or Miele. Dun & Bradstreet's key business ratios show whether Maytag's numbers are among the top quartile, median, or bottom quartile of the field. Using these ratios, one can prove factually Maytag's profitability in relation to its competitors and in relation to other unrelated industries.

But how does one compare the service given by a Maytag repairman with the service given by a British Airways stewardess or the service given by a counter clerk at McDonald's? There are no standard concrete measurements and no Dun & Bradstreet books to guide us—yet.

FUTURE MEASUREMENT

The process of installing concrete measurement standards, however, has begun and is well under way. At a Marriott hotel, for example, guests find a card to order breakfast and hang outside the door before retiring. The card states a service guarantee. If Marriott delivers a guest's breakfast more than 15 minutes late, the breakfast is free. In this way, Marriott is giving birth to a concrete measurement of customer service in the hotel industry for the delivery of room service breakfasts. Perhaps key service ratios will soon be published that show, for the hotel industry, the percentage of room service breakfasts served on time or within a 15-minute tolerance by the top quartile, median, and bottom quartile performers.

But, at present, there are no concrete measurements proving that to be highly profitable, a company or organization must deliver superior customer service. Other factors cloud the issue:

- If all the companies or organizations in a particular field are offering mediocre or poor customer service, there is often no catalyst for change. All of the companies or organizations in this field can be profitable without making customer service improvements. If none of the competitors "rock the boat," if consumers find equal dissatisfaction with all companies in the field, and if consumers do not find ways of comparing the service levels in this field with service levels in other fields, the situation can continue.

- Like all factors affecting profitability, overriding market or world economy factors can cause a company or organization to be profitable while delivering mediocre or poor customer service or be unprofitable while delivering superior customer service. If the dollar is suddenly strong against the British pound, a superior customer service company with operations in the United States and United Kingdom can watch its British profits translated to lower U.S. profits.

- Many would argue that some customer service factors can never be quantified. What ratios would measure, for example, the degree of empathy displayed by one company's mail order clerk versus a competitor's mail order clerk when a customer complains that the dress she ordered for a special occasion didn't fit when it arrived and came too late for alterations? Until such factors are translated into measurable factors, good or bad customer service will be a subjective and sometimes emotional rating.

- Monopolies exist. They can deliver terrible service but be very profitable.

- Nonprofit organizations also engage in service delivery, both good and bad. Most of these organizations have some measure of success other than profit. Contribution goals are an obvious measure of success.

- Timing is a factor, as is the problem of evaluating short-term versus long-term profits. If a company's customer service levels deteriorate and customers turn to competitors, swift cost-reduction measures or prompt actions to sign up new customers can prevent the deterioration in service from showing on the bottom line. But when there are no further cost-reduction measures to take or new customers to sign up, the impact will fall to the bottom line.

QUALITY

Philip Crosby, in his book *Quality Is Free* (1979), concretely defines quality, whether in manufacturing or service, as "doing things right the first time. Quality means conformance, not elegance."

While many organizations today may not be convinced that the quality of service they offer impacts bottom-line performance, Crosby states quite clearly: "Quality is not only free, it is an honest-to-everything profit maker. Every penny you don't spend on doing things wrong, over, or instead becomes half a penny right on the bottom line."

In *Time* magazine's February 2, 1987, cover story, "Why Is Service So Bad?" Stephen Koepp says: "Quality service gurus like John Tshohl of Bloomington, Minn., are now in heavy demand to give speeches to top managers. Says he: 'We teach them the financial impact of good customer service. They're interested only in hard dollars and cents.'"

Peters and Waterman in their book, *In Search of Excellence* (1982), state that "service, quality, reliability are strategies aimed at loyalty and long-term revenue stream growth (and maintenance)." They describe the total dedication of Frito-Lay, a subsidiary of PepsiCo, to its sales force. "It will spend several hundred dollars sending a truck to restock a store with a couple of $30 cartons of potato chips" in order to uphold its "99.5 percent service level." Yet Frito-Lay "sells well over $2 billion worth of potato chips and pretzels each year, owns market shares that run into the 60s and 70s in most of the country, and has margins that are the envy of the food industry."

While there is no definitive empirical data to support an absolute link between customer service and profitability, current and recent best-sellers provide many convincing examples and principles; for example, *In Search of Excellence* (1982); *Service America,* by Karl Albrecht and Ron Zemke (1985); *The 100 Best Companies to Work for in America,* by Robert Levering, Milton Moskowitz, and Michael Katz (1984); *The Journey to Excellence,* by Mike Robson (1986); several books on quality by Philip Crosby, and even the previously mentioned *Time* cover story. Excellent studies and research programs have also been undertaken by Technical Assistance Research Programs, Inc. (TARP), of Washington, D.C. In all, an entire body of convincing material produced by experts supports the theory that customer service and profitability are linked. In addition, an array of consulting firms, like Time Manager International (Copenhagen and New York) have sprung to life and thrive on providing customer service guidance and training to companies and organizations.

REALITY AND PERFORMANCE

Despite the growing evidence that good customer service affects the bottom line, each day around the world thousands of employees go to work to face customers and deliver mediocre or poor service. Each day thousands of employees go to work to sit in offices where they never speak to a customer, and never once think about a customer in regard to their work. Each day thousands of middle managers manage these employees, condoning by their very presence mediocre or poor service or total lack of concern for customers. And each day hundreds of chief executives and senior managers spend long hours in meetings, analyzing numbers, making massive short-range and long-range decisions, planning strategies, speaking to the press, fending off takeovers, lining up financing, but never talking about the service their companies deliver to customers.

Why? How can all that is written and discussed on the links between service, quality, reliability, and profitability be so routinely ignored by so many? Here are some of the common excuses:

- "Our company is very profitable, three percent more profitable than predicted. No more customer complaint letters seem to be coming in than last year."

- "So one area did a survey and found that our front-line employees are apathetic. How do we know that isn't an improvement over last year?"

- "Customer complaint letters in the last fiscal year totaled 100,000. At the running rate so far this year, we're at only 90 percent of last year. So our service is getting better."

- "Our pricing and our products are equal to or superior to those of our competitors."

- "We already have a 60 percent share of market."

- "Of course customer service is important. But we must prevent a hostile takeover of our company, and that demands a great deal of our time."

- "The last time I did what I thought was right for a customer, my manager wasn't happy about it."

- "We're trying to reduce the cost of our receivables here. That's what I'm paid to do."

- "I keep submitting proposals to improve customer service, but I never hear anything back."

- "Customer service? Oh, yes, we have a whole department called that. It's run by that new man, er, I don't recall his name."

- "It's very hard to get people to stay for very long in our front-line jobs. They have to do shift work. So we're forced to employ many people who don't have the right attitude about service."

- "We'd like to reward our employees on the basis of service delivered in addition to revenue, productivity, and share of market growth. But we simply don't have the systems to measure it."

- "They trained me to work the computer system really well. But they didn't train me to deal with customers."

- "It's against the rules for me to do everything the customer wants."

These excuses are the reasons this book has ten more chapters. In them, readers will find examples, both good and bad, guidelines, and practical advice on how to give superior customer service from the front-line, from the back office, from middle management, and from the boardroom.

2

It Starts with Commitment

In the center of the picturesque Austrian ski resort of Seefeld in the Tirol stands the Hotel Klosterbraeu, owned and managed by the Seyrling family. During the 110-day winter season, the hotel enjoys an occupancy rate of 87 percent to 89 percent; for the 110-day summer season, the occupancy rate is 80 percent. The hotel capacity is 220 overnight guests, with ample facilities for conferences, banquets, and balls. At any given point, 80 percent of the guests are returning guests who've stayed there before. Some of them feel the Klosterbraeu is one of the world's best hotels.

For the past 28 seasons, Simo Vujicic has worked at the hotel, leaving his home in Yugoslavia for each 110-day season. He started as a dishwasher and is now the night porter. Three other members of his family work there too, including a porter employed for 16 years.

In the wee hours of the morning, Simo is the only staff member on duty to cater to every need, from medical emergencies, to lovers' quarrels, to the odd 4:00 A.M. request for food or drink. He also handles the wake-up calls to all guests and to members of the Seyrling family. Mrs. Midi Seyrling says proudly that in 14 years, she has "not had one single complaint. Simo has awakened all guests and every member of the Seyrling family always on time."

With these compliments, Simo will smile and blush. He believes he is just doing his job. He is characteristic of the hotel's 170 staff members, of which 70 to 80 change each year. While a frequent guest can identify new employees from the "old hands" and from members of the Seyrling family, a new guest cannot, for all staff members display the same commitment and belief that it is "all just part of the job."

The job to these employees is simply to do whatever is necessary to make the guests have a happy and memorable stay. From the dishwasher to the general manager, this is exactly how each staff member views the job. This is commitment.

GOING CONCERN PRINCIPLE

In the most elementary accounting courses, students learn basic concepts, including the "going concern principle." This concept says simply that most businesses begin with the basic idea that they will be operated in a logical, rational manner that will lead to success over an extended period of time.

If one were thinking of setting up a new business, the goal would probably be to make a profit over a period of time. To achieve this primary goal one would probably have a set of principles or a philosophy about operating the business. One of these principles might include giving good customer service. A sign or poster somewhere on the business premises might display the commitment to customers, and it might appear in promotional literature.

In fact, in almost all companies and organizations, a sign or poster somewhere makes a statement about customer service. Signs show that "we aim to please," "the customer is always right," and "the customer is number one."

Each day around the world, millions of ordinary people deliver superior customer service. Each day millions of ordinary people deliver ordinary service. And each day millions of people deliver poor or inconsistent service. Yet many of these people are standing beside signs that say their aim is to give good customer service. How can this happen?

COMMITMENT SLUMP FACTORS

If a business intends to make a profit and includes good customer service in its set of principles, what could happen to alter its commitment? Following are some of the most common causes:

1. The business might become a monopoly or be doing business in a marketplace where all competitors offer mediocre, poor, or inconsistent service. The financial staff could easily recommend and get agreement to cost reduction measures that reduced service delivery.

2. The business might be offering a product for which there is heavy demand or, in economic terms, there is overdemand and undersupply. A good example of this was seen in 1987 in the U.S. airline industry. Overdemand and undersupply occur routinely in some businesses, such as facilities for wedding receptions in June.

3. Management changes in various areas of the organization, particularly those that occur without orientation or initial training, or in the top levels of the organization can alter customer service delivery.

4. Ownership changes can also alter the commitment to customer service.

5. As employees generally tend to be the deliverers of service, radical staff changes can also have an effect. Excessive turnover, particularly coupled with insufficient training, or significant changes in employees' compensation packages can bring change.

6. Even though a strong commitment may exist at the top of the organization, variations of the principles may be applied in isolated parts of the business, particularly if some business is done far from the main office. Segments of the business might even operate at cross purposes.

7. The business might grow so quickly as to require investment of more money to expand facilities and production. During this time, concern with expansion may overtake the commitment to customer service. In fact, almost any widespread or radical change creates an opportunity for service to suffer.

8. If any part of the business involves employing artistic talent or highly qualified professionals, the business might overconcentrate on artistic flourish or academic accomplishment to the detriment of customer service.

9. New government controls or the removal of government controls could affect customer service either by direct intervention or indirect impact. When the Spanish government raised the tax from 15 percent to 33 percent on some tourist services, some of the businesses affected concentrated on adjustments to their billing and accounting systems without considering easily predictable problems such as foreign tourists not having enough money with them to pay for these items.

10. Businesses involving product manufacture could make a bad or faulty product. In the pharmaceutical industry, the product might even be dangerous. While problems should create an opportunity for customer service principles to shine, a slump in commitment could occur in the rush to correct the error.

11. Total automation or total standardization or robotization of service delivery might seem to eliminate the need to deliver good service, or one might operate under this belief.

12. As profits increased the business might become selfcongratulatory and lose touch with the service actually being delivered or with the service customers now want.

Obviously, one would want to protect a business from slumps in commitment. But as modern businesses grow in size and complexity, they fall into these traps with increasing frequency. Few businesses make a deliberate decision to offer poor service. But at all levels of the organization, no matter what the business or industry, there is a need to recognize the signals of a slump in commitment and what can change the course.

COMMITMENT SLUMP SIGNALS

The most obvious signal of a slump in commitment to superior service is measured service deterioration. Measured service deterioration can show up in the revenue and profit lines or in formal measurement programs such as an increase in customer complaint letters and telephone calls or lower scores or ratings on quality assurance reports. Measured service deterioration can be uncovered in marketing research or can even be reported by front-line service employees.

In an organization in which all levels share the dedication to superior service, these types of measurements are used and studied frequently, and the slightest deterioration prompts immediate investigation and remedial action. In an organization less committed to superior service, these measurements might generate excuses such as:

- "Revenues are down 2 percent due to pricing actions and the Memorial Day weekend."

- "Customer complaint telephone calls have increased since we printed the toll-free complaint number on all invoices."

- "The quality assurance reports show a lower score this month due to increased volumes and also because of the damage we suffered during the hurricane."

- "The market research findings were affected by our decision to pull our television ads just before the research was done."

- "The employees in our Seattle branch say there's bad customer reaction to our new campaign, but then there has been some union organizing activity out there recently, and they don't really have any statistics to back up their claims."

These excuses may, of course, be valid reasons for changes in performance. However, in a truly service-committed organization, they will be examined and reexamined to make sure that this is the case.

In some organizations, neither partial nor complete formal measurements exist. Measurement of customer complaints, for example, may have been eliminated due to headcount constraints or may have been made too costly to function by a change in operation. For example, a company with operations in 130 countries introduced a new billing and receivables system whereby customers were billed by the operation in their country of residence rather than by the operation in the country where they used the service. As a result, complaints were directed to the office in the customer's country of residence, and the office in the country where the service was used often did not know of complaints.

Despite much focus on customer service in newspapers, magazines, books, and advertising, many companies and organizations have not yet developed a service philosophy or guidelines. These organizations have no measurement and no way of knowing when service deteriorates or when commitment changes.

Cost-reduction measures, particularly those that affect service levels, may be indirect signals of a slump in commitment to superior service. The most noticeable signals are staffing reductions in the customer complaint department or in any service-delivery function. As allocation of funds to serving customers indicates that management wants to achieve superior service, so it follows that a reduction in these funds signals a lowering of standards. Management reluctance to approve new service offerings, to conduct market research on customer needs, or to devote funds to new product offerings indicates decline in service delivery expectations. Obsession and preoccupation with pricing, production, financing, takeovers, and ownership changes or inattention to the service being delivered are also warning signs.

Less obvious signals include the reluctance to spend time or money to fix recurring problems. The Internal Revenue Service shows this reluctance in its customer complaint form. A form just makes it easier for the customer to complain. The process may also include a form letter to answer the customer's complaint.

Another warning is reluctance to fix problems arising elsewhere in the organization or seeing problems as being outside the organization's control. If an airport authority forbids large directional signs, car rental companies must then live with small signs and confused customers. Or, are there service alternatives?

OPPORTUNITIES FOR SERVICE

Commitment, whether personal and emotional or of the organization's funds, is affected by the circumstances in which service is delivered and the opportunities it allows for service to occur.

Some service situations appear to be well defined and intensely regulated. If a customer goes to McDonald's for a Big Mac, fries, and a Coke, he expects these standard products to be delivered quickly and politely in clean surroundings at the McDonald's price. In this situation, the employee has little opportunity for creativity. The customer's only expectation of an automated teller machine is that a check-cashing transaction with a machine will result in the receipt of money from an account.

Other service situations, however, require far more exercise of service skills. If a patient is being told that he needs open-heart surgery, the doctor delivering this news and performing the surgery had better look and act like the world's greatest heart surgeon and be able to explain everything—from the operating procedure to the size of the bedpans—like the world's greatest instructor with heavenly powers on her side. If a patron visits a hairdresser before an important engagement, the hairdresser needs to have the skills—both technical skills and customer service skills—to convince the patron that she looks her best when she leaves the premises.

A committed service organization views all situations in which customer and organization come into contact as crucial opportunities for service performance or, as Jan Carlzon of SAS calls them, "moments of truth."

At the McDonald's in Bracknell, England, the milkshake machine was broken for several days. Rather than meeting harassed employees, customers were treated to employees who cheerfully recommended every other drink McDonald's had to offer. When the restaurant ran out of ketchup, customers were enthusiastically offered mustard sauce, curry sauce, or sweet and sour sauce for their fries.

During construction at Houston's Hobby Airport in 1981, car rental customers faced a long, dark, unguided trek through the construction site to the rental cars, which were all parked together in unmarked spaces. This 20- to 30-minute ordeal completely negated the pleasant and efficient two- or three-minute rental procedure at the airport rental counter, yet no car rental company seized the opportunity to post a guide and distinguish itself as a superior service company.

Without a service philosophy or a sense of mission, an organization turns service opportunities into service ordeals. Commitment to superior service, on the other hand, can make an impossible situation a bearable or even a memorable service event.

REPUTATION

Some organizations continue to prosper under superior service reputations earned many years ago. Harrod's Department Store in London is such an example.

It seems logical to believe that it takes a long time to build a good reputation for service, but if service deteriorates, the news will spread fast. Yet this is not always the case. Faster global communication speeds the news of outstanding service. Frequent customers notice and talk about dramatic changes in service delivery. Advertising provides a means only of reaching infrequent and prospective customers.

When service deteriorates, however, several factors may help the organization rest on its reputation. Clever marketing and advertising slogans, campaigns, and programs may still be remembered by customers, particularly by infrequent customers. These same slogans, campaigns, and programs may also be remembered by long-serving employees who still make every effort to deliver superior service. Top management's decline in service commitment does not necessarily mean that the entire organization has lost this goal. Isolated units may still be keenly interested in service delivery.

In the famous food halls at Harrod's it is possible to be ignored for over twenty minutes when trying to make a purchase and for a customer to be "told off" for being unaware of the new take-a-number system at the cheese counter. Yet it is also possible for customers to watch their meat orders being cut and packaged by a butcher who takes great pride and care in the process and who even carries purchases to customers' cars.

CONSISTENCY

Related to reputation is consistency in both commitment and service delivery.

Consistency is a key element in the selection and continued listing of restaurants and hotels in guidebooks and ratings such as those produced by Michelin (1981). Michelin relies not only on the regular visits to restaurants and hotels by their inspectors but also on comments by users of the guides. As stated in the opening: "Your opinions, whether praising or criticizing, are welcomed and will be examined on the spot by our inspectors in order to make our Guide even better."

Consistency is a critical element in service delivery. Perhaps because it disappoints high expectations, inconsistent service is perceived by customers as worse than overall poor service.

Inconsistent service may provoke truly violent customer reaction. The confirmed hotel room that isn't available upon arrival because of overbooking, the inedible anniversary dinner in a recommended restaurant, the backed-up toilet that the regular plumber is unable to fix when one has a house full of guests, provide disproportionate irritation.

MARKET CHANGES

Superior customer service depends on keeping a constant eye on market changes. A company or organization slow to react to market demand may lack commitment to superior service. Marketing research firms exist because of the ever-present danger that there is a difference between what customers really want and what the company believes its customers really want.

Market factors are at work in the successful and rapidly expanding position of Domino's Pizza in 1987 vis-à-vis Pizza Hut. Starting with the rather spartan down-market appeal of going out for a pizza, Pizza Hut has turned the pizza parlor into a pleasant family restaurant. Domino's instead has targeted itself at that segment of the market that used to go into a local pizza parlor for carry out or that used to call the local pizza parlor for pizza delivery. While Pizza Hut also delivers pizzas, Domino's pizza delivery system is recognized as the service leader. But both companies must watch the pizza marketplace carefully for changes. If, for example, eating a pizza at home were to become suddenly unfashionable, Domino's guarantee of speedy delivery would become meaningless to customers.

The commitment to respond to market changes must also extend beyond the control a company believes it has if it is to be perceived as delivering superior service.

Crego's Shoe Store in the city center of Harrisburg, Pennsylvania, has long been known for quality. It offers personalized, professional, and friendly service and sells quality products in a variety of price ranges. As the city center declined in the 1970s, most stores moved to urban shopping malls. While most shoppers had been willing to pay for parking in the city center when they were shopping at a wide variety of stores, they were less willing to pay to shop in the few stores left. Crego's outstanding service reputation kept loyal patrons, but it was losing ground. The market demanded that Crego's do more outside the scope of selling shoes.

Crego's now offers customers free parking while they are shopping in its store, validating the parking entry ticket for the most convenient city parking area. Rather than moving to a shopping mall or going out of business like other stores, Crego's does business from its normal site and has even expanded into women's and men's clothing.

TRANSLATING COMMITMENT INTO ACTION

Commitment is a feeling, but the feeling has definite and tangible signs. If a person became committed to learning to ski, he would spend money planning a vacation to a place offering lessons, he would spend money on ski equipment and ski clothes, and would talk about skiing with friends. After the vacation, he would talk about his progress in learning to ski, show photographs and talk about good times, and might buy more ski equipment and ski clothes and start planning for the next ski trip. He might dream about skiing the Matterhorn, but when he stood awkwardly for the first time on a pair of skis, he'd point to the nearest "big" slope (i.e., one that looks enormous to a beginner but one that most ski instructors know a beginner can ski after a few days of good instruction) and declare that after so many days, he'd like to be able to ski down it. And he would.

Commitment to delivering superior service is expressed and translated into action in much the same way. People have to talk about it with enthusiasm, to spend money on doing it, and to have small successes (i.e., "big" slopes) along the way. While the return on investment from a commitment to learning to ski is enjoyment and personal achievement, the return on investment from the commitment to delivering superior service will be measured in terms of increased revenues, increased profits, and reduced costs as well as happier employees and happier customers.

In most organizations having successfully executed a long-range superior service commitment, the commitment began near or at the top of the organization and has been led on a long-range basis from the top. But this commitment has quickly spread to all areas of the organization.

The journey to service excellence is almost always a long and continuing process. It seldom has an end.

A commitment to superior service might begin with an action plan to implement two services based on market research of what customers wanted. In an independent hotel, for example, management could initiate a service guarantee of delivering room service breakfasts on time, offering free breakfast if it were delivered more than ten minutes late. Second might be a teletext check-out that enabled guests using accepted credit cards to review and approve their hotel bill via the television set in their rooms and simply pick up a copy of the charges at a special location as they left the hotel. Management's dedication to the plan would be shown by funding to conduct the market research and to draw up and execute these two services, as well as the resources to specify the costs of introducing the services and to estimate the expected return on investment. Funding would also cover the cost of evaluative measurements of the services' success.

Once a successful action has been taken and the results measured, a pattern exists for further successes. But they don't happen automatically. Commitment must remain strong at the top of the organization and flow through to all other areas.

THE NEED FOR A CRISIS

It seems relatively straightforward and do-able to begin a commitment to superior service and to translate it into action. Yet many organizations never try, or their attempts fail.

A common reason for failure is that the commitment is weak. Just allocating funding and resources to improving service delivery is insufficient. Management and employees at all levels have to be so dedicated to superior service that it shows in virtually all of their business actions.

If the chief executives of all the world's companies and organizations that deliver service in any way, shape, or form, were gathered together and asked to raise their hands if they believed in giving good customer service, as many hands would be raised as if a convention of people were asked to raise their hands if they liked sex. Everyone believes in good customer service, both giving it and receiving it. But an organization needs to know the strength of its determination to spend money and change the way it delivers service.

A common cause of weak commitment, or of strong verbal commitment without the devotion of management time, resources, or funding, is the feeling that everything is basically okay. There is no crisis. Why risk radical change if profits are good?

In truth, when customer service is poor a crisis does exist, but only some people see it. If the battleground of the past for companies has been to produce a quality product at the right price in response to market demand, the battleground of today and tomorrow is service—how to get the product into the hands of customers and how to get customers to successfully use the product and repeat their business. Just as consumers will pay a premium price for a premium product, so will they pay a premium price for premium service.

One successful technique for opening eyes at the top of the organization is to manufacture a crisis. Chief executives often manage from crisis to crisis. If they see no crisis in service delivery, they will give it lower priority than whatever crisis is at hand.

Manufacturing a crisis does not mean misrepresenting the facts. Rather it is combining facts in such a way as to show the magnitude of the threat and thus the strength of the opportunity. Following is an example of such a crisis.

A company conducts about 479,000 transactions a year with

customers, each transaction representing about $100 in revenue and $17 in operating profit. Written letters of complaint received this year are 28,740, which is slightly lower than the previous year. Everything is okay.

But telephone calls of complaint, letters of complaint, and verbal complaints in person are being received and dealt with at 60 outlying locations and in five head office departments other than the customer service department, and these are not counted in the 28,740. A conservative estimate is that for every letter of complaint received by the customer service department, two additional complaints are not counted. Also, market research shows that 28 percent of those who write a letter of complaint to the customer service department switch brands because of poor service.

The picture is now that complaints are 86,220, or 18 percent of transactions, and 24,142 of these will switch brands. At this rate, the revenue loss in one year is $2,414,200, the profit loss $410,414. But these customers could have been expected to do 1.2 transactions a year with the company, so the total loss over the next 20 years is $9,849,936 in operating profit at today's prices. This is a crisis.

The top executives of many organizations think in terms of numbers and specifically in numbers relating to profit. Like other activities in a corporation such as manufacturing or marketing, customer service must be expressed in numbers that relate to profit. Each service idea must be expressed in terms of the cost of executing it and the expected return on investment it will bring. Without this, the crisis is not apparent and commitment may not occur.

GUIDELINES FOR CHIEF EXECUTIVES

At every level of the organization, employees believe the chief executive has the power to make superior service or poor service happen, and that if the chief executive is committed to delivering superior service, it will happen.

However, many chief executives have to answer to stockholders, to parent companies, to boards of directors, to potential owners, to patrons and financiers, to the public, even to heads of governments, and the most common topic of conversation with these people is profit—dividends, earnings per share, profit growth, and so on. Superior service goals must be expressed in terms of profit.

While chief executives may feel their limited executive time should be devoted to serious threats such as hostile takeovers, they do possess the power to command the total company's resources, if necessary, to look at service delivery and provide recommendations, complete with an estimate of return on investment.

A chief executive would have the power to ask, for example, "How much more profit would we earn if we reduced our number of dissatisfied customers by 2 percent?" or "How much more profit would we earn if we introduced a service our competitors don't offer now and would be slow to copy?"

The answers to these questions exist or can be found in most companies, and chief executives need to ask them. Chief executives do have the power to initiate and reinforce programs and actions aimed at delivering superior service. Chief executives should ask themselves the following questions:

1. If I am anywhere near a point where my company is delivering service, even if only for a moment, do I observe and notice how service is being delivered and do I take action on anything that is wrong?

2. How many days in the last year have I actually spent working as a customer contact employee in my company?

3. How many hours in the last twelve months have I spent actually talking to my company's customers?

4. Do I know the reasons why customers are dissatisfied with the service my company provides? Do I know how much it would cost to correct each of the major sources of dissatisfaction?

5. Do I know exactly how many customers are dissatisfied with the service my company provides and how much it costs to handle this dissatisfaction?

6. Do I know exactly how many of my dissatisfied customers switch to using competitors and how much profit the company will lose because of this?

The only unacceptable answers are "no" and "none." All other answers indicate a need to reevaluate service goals.

The following statements in *Business Life* magazine by Frank Olsen, chief executive at Allegis and long-time chief executive of Hertz, are thought provoking:

Generally when I travel, I work. International flights I try to use like an office. I get properly organized and try to forget where I am. One of my pet peeves in that respect is, I'm afraid, other people. If you really have a lot of work planned, there's little more irritating than getting everything prepared and having the guy next to you say, 'And what do you do?' Particularly in my business, I used to try and be polite and say that I worked for Hertz, only to be greeted with the story of a dirty car in Chicago. But I think I've found the answer. Now I say I work for Avis and then when I get the story of the dirty car in Chicago I just say, 'I know, it's a lousy company; that's why I'm quitting.'

Frank Olsen, *Business Life* Magazine, August/September 1987

These statements by a chief executive set the tone of commitment and service strategy for an entire organization—in this case, one of admitting failure and having no solution in sight. As a story at a cocktail party, it's amusing. But as a statement in print, it's an enormous opportunity for competitors.

GUIDELINES FOR FRONT-LINE SERVICE DELIVERY PERSONNEL

A company's chief executive and senior management team have power, high salaries, and benefits, but the service is handled by front-line service delivery personnel. To the customer *they* are the company.

In many companies, front-line service delivery personnel work undesirable hours for low pay, receive insufficient training, and must follow many rules and policies with little freedom or the necessary tools to satisfy customers' needs. Yet their customers expect superior service.

Applicants for or employees in service delivery jobs must understand that serving customers is the primary function. The employer may not reward exceptional service behavior or may not promote people because they have given superior customer service, but other factors should influence these employees. If one has to spend one-third of each 24-hour period serving customers, or one-half of waking time, then this time should be as enjoyable as possible. A satisfied customer may be the only reward.

The economy of Austria's western region depends heavily on tourism. Guenther Oelhafen began working as a management trainee at the five-star Hotel Europa in Innsbruck when he was 17. He learned the business from the ground up, cheerfully carrying bags for people from many different countries, always giving pleasant advice even to customers tired and difficult after a long journey. An American family once reminisced with Guenther about a special homemade Apfelstruedel (apple strudel) they had once had. Guenther brought them another Apfelstruedel made by his own grandmother. While the hotel prided itself on its five-star service, Guenther saw his own satisfaction in giving customers good service and helpful advice. When a friend in the travel trade asked Guenther to look after a Japanese visitor for two days, he did just that, taking care of the visitor in the hotel and showing him around Innsbruck on his own time. The next year found Guenther on a two-week dream holiday in Japan with the Japanese visitor rolling out the red carpet for him.

Not all customers reward so generously. Some may not even seem to notice efforts in their behalf. A few may even go away angry because the person they encountered did not have the power to solve their problems. But front-line service deliverers should ask themselves daily:

1. Do I believe in the company I work for, its product, and the service I am giving?

2. Do I listen to customers who have a problem, a question, or a special request and try to understand what they want?

3. Do I empathize with customers who have a problem, a question, or a special request and verify what they would like to have?

4. Do I take action to solve problems, answer questions, and handle special requests?

5. Do I shoulder the blame for any inconvenience or misunderstanding caused by other areas of my organization or by customers themselves?

6. Do I do everything within my power to satisfy the needs of each and every customer and treat each and every customer as an individual?

7. Do I recommend service enhancement ideas to my supervisor or manager?

The acceptable answer to all of these questions has to be "yes."

GUIDELINES FOR BACK-OFFICE SERVICE SUPPORT PERSONNEL

Like front-line service delivery personnel, back-office service support personnel often suffer from the same low pay, undesirable working hours, insufficient training, and proliferation of rules and policies to follow with little freedom for personal initiative. Almost any error made by service support personnel—such as posting a payment to the wrong account, manufacturing a faulty product, or writing an incorrect procedure into a company manual—is felt by front-line service delivery personnel who may even have to shoulder the blame for the error. But while front-line service delivery personnel have the opportunity to feel the warmth of a satisfied customer's smile or to hear sincere words of thanks, the back-office support employee often lacks even these opportunities.

Employees in any service support position, at any level, need to keep in mind how exactly their job relates to the company's customers and ask themselves the following questions:

1. Do I know exactly how my job relates to the product and/or service my company gives and can I readily explain this to others?

2. Do I do everything within my power to perform my job so that the needs of each and every customer are satisfied?

3. Do I believe in the company I work for, its product, and the importance of the job I'm doing for the customer?

4. Do I do everything within my power to make the job of the service delivery personnel as successful as possible?

5. Do I recommend ways of doing my job to my supervisor or manager so that customers receive better service?

Again, the acceptable answer to all of these questions has to be "yes."

GUIDELINES FOR MIDDLE MANAGEMENT

In the service environment, middle management is those persons who manage service delivery and service support personnel, without being in routine contact with customers themselves, but who are not the chief executive or part of the chief executive's inner circle of key senior executives. Middle management forms the link between the people who cause superior, mediocre, or poor service to happen—both service delivery and service support personnel— and the top of the organization that communicates overall goals, leads corporate direction, and prioritizes strategies.

While many members of middle management might say they are operating in an ill-defined arena with little power, in truth this group can squash or carry forward service enhancement ideas from service delivery and service support personnel; give lip service to or ardently implement the orders of the chief executive; or provide opportunities that deeply depress or strongly motivate service delivery and service support personnel. In short, this group has enormous power over service quality. Yet individual managers frequently say, "Yes, we should improve our quality of service, but what can I do?"

Middle managers often have the opportunity to try out and test new service ideas in their own operating unit and then report the successes to the rest of the organization. As a group banding itself together across multiple disciplines, middle management can create the synergy and impetus to get ideas approved and implemented.

Middle managers need to ask themselves:

1. Do I believe in the company I work for, its product, and the service being given to customers?

2. Do I encourage and listen to ideas from service delivery and service support personnel, help to refine, quantify, and cost-justify them, and bring them to the attention of the decision-makers in the organization in the ways most likely to gain approval?

3. Do I make every effort to fully understand corporate goals, directions, and strategies and to execute them in concert with their intent?

4. Do I provide opportunities for service delivery and service support personnel to perform their jobs well and to feel some initiative and positive rewards in service-related situations?

5. Do I schedule myself regularly to work as a customer contact employee in my company, to speak to my company's customers, and to listen to service delivery and service support personnel?

Middle managers need to shout a chorus of "yes" to these questions. They hold the key to executing superior service programs.

A FEW LAST WORDS ON COMMITMENT

Get some. Get as much as possible. Get others to get it, too.

3

Get the Right People to Deliver Service

Maureen was an instructor for Avis in the Chicago training center. Much of her time was spent conducting a two-week intensive program for newly hired rental sales agents from the Midwest. In one of her student groups was a quiet young woman from Kansas City. Maureen watched Sarah very carefully, but it was apparent that Sarah was understanding and grasping the technical aspects of the job well. She didn't respond to questions in the classroom even though her work indicated she knew the answers. Nor did she talk with fellow students during coffee breaks and lunches.

At lunch one day, Maureen asked Sarah some direct questions. Sarah replied with painful shyness and reluctance. Yes, she was enjoying the training course and liked Avis so far. She liked her fellow students and the instructor. She just didn't like talking to people.

HIRING WARM BODIES

Customer contact employees are often on the low end of the pay scale in service companies. This work force can be generally characterized as low-paid, young, inexperienced in the business environment, forced to work undesirable shifts, and quick to change jobs. Given such high turnover, even in areas with high unemployment, coupled with the need to replace quickly, many front-line managers readily admit that they hire "warm bodies": any person who is willing to take the job.

The practice of hiring warm bodies creates a continuing spiral with much synergy. Such new employees create a drain on existing staff, generating even more turnover. Everybody races to keep the business going, despite heavy absenteeism, high turnover, and lack of knowledge and experience. The strain is apparent to customers, and service levels deteriorate. Since turnover and absenteeism are recognized cost factors, revenue and profit performance often deteriorate as well. There are no candidates for promotion to supervisory and management positions, and everyone feels stress.

Managers at any level in this spiral have difficulty stepping back and looking at the root causes and what can be done to stop the spiral. But that objectivity is imperative and solutions are often difficult. In many cases managers know what the solutions are, but are unable to implement them. Consider the problems of the manager of a small gift shop in a hotel. The sales staff consists of four young men and women who rotate shifts to cover all the hours that the gift shop is open. One calls in sick just before his shift. The manager must get one of the other three to cover that shift, or take it herself. Simultaneously, another employee gives the manager her two-week notice. In addition to covering the shifts of the sick employee, the manager has to find a new employee and run the business, not to mention keeping a watchful eye on the soon-to-depart employee who has now taken to showing up late, leaving early, and boasting to the other two employees about her new job, the better pay and hours she'll enjoy, and how easy it would be for them to do the same. The employment agency has only one suitable candidate who can start on the necessary date. She makes a nice appearance, seems intelligent, and has previously worked in a gift shop. The only drawback is that she doesn't like to talk to people. Will the manager hire this warm body to reduce her own stress?

JOB DESCRIPTIONS AND PERSON SPECIFICATIONS

The solutions to the synergistic downward spiral of hiring inappropriate employees start with the basics. Managers must first have a clear idea of the job to be done and the skills required to do it. Job applicants need to know what the job is and whether they have the skills to do it.

The format and presentation of these ideas are not important, but rather the thought process that goes into making up the job description and into determining which skills are necessary for successful performance.

Job descriptions are often viewed as a time-consuming exercise that produces something nobody but the personnel department ever reads. They are often out-of-date soon after they're written. Sometimes the sole purpose of the job description is to give personnel a justification for giving the job a higher grading, a higher salary, or better benefits.

But despite the frustrations in writing job descriptions, the fact remains that to employ a person to do a job, one has to know what that job is. A good job description is the way to do this, whether it takes the form of bullet points on a paper napkin or a highly formatted printed booklet.

JOB DESCRIPTIONS FOR CUSTOMER CONTACT EMPLOYEES

One of the most useful ways to begin the thought process behind writing a job description is to ask, "Why does this job exist?" The answer to this question should result in one sentence or phrase that describes the overall function of the job. It also should include why the job is important to the company or organization.

Following are examples of one-sentence descriptions:

1. To provide in-flight service to passengers so that they will want to fly with this airline again.

2. To wash and service cars so that they operate safely and comfortably and customers will want to rent them again.

3. To help callers with their questions and problems so that they'll be able to complete their income tax forms accurately and on time.

4. To help customers buy what they need and to help customers select gifts that they are proud to give so that customers will spend more money in this gift shop.

5. To style, cut, and arrange customers' hair so that they feel good about how they look and will return for further visits.

6. To repair television sets so that customers are satisfied and will call this repair service for any further breakdowns.

7. To handle thirty calls per hour so that twenty of them result in bookings and so that customers will want to call this service for further bookings and information.

In all of these examples is a mercenary element: the jobs exist to serve customers so that customers will use the product or service again. As most companies or organizations exist to make a profit, there is no harm in this honesty. "We're doing it this way to get customers to willingly spend their money with us again and again." Even in government and nonprofit organizations, job functions normally have an income element. If the job is to help people prepare income tax forms, the goal is to see that they do it accurately and on time so that the government will receive its correct income on time without the cost of auditing returns or handling late returns.

Even in areas that customers do not think of positively in terms of repeat business, such as repair services and medical services, capturing repeat business is still a goal, but its presentation to customers must be tactful.

The "why" part of job statements also carries an element of accountability. Customer contact employees are indeed accountable for bringing customers back, along with other employees such as the ones who manufacture and control the quality of a product. To deliver superior service and gain repeat business and brand loyalty, accountability must be spread into each employee's job description.

Typical job descriptions next set out the job duties. This enumeration can be detailed or broad. What is important is to state the elements of the job so that the employee or applicant will understand what is expected of him or her. Good descriptions of job duties include measures of accountability or measurements of success that tell employees how they will know when they've been successful in carrying out each duty.

A third element of many job descriptions is a list of the skills required to do the job. These generally follow logically from the statement of why the job exists and the description of the duties. However, in many companies a description of the skills required for customer contact employees would include detailed and specific requirements of technical skills and less detailed and less specific requirements of service skills. It is easier to say, "types at a speed of 70 words per minute with no errors" than to say, "answers the telephone and handles incoming calls in such a way that callers feel satisfied their call has been handled professionally, pleasantly, and efficiently." Also, it is easier to evaluate whether a prospective applicant for a secretarial position can type at a speed of 70 words per minute with no errors than whether the prospective applicant is professional, pleasant, and efficient at handling incoming telephone calls. Training, of course, can provide some of these skills, but some must exist at the start. While good typing skill can be acquired without a particular attitude, service skill almost always requires service attitudes, and these are not easily trained. But difficulty in defining and evaluating service skills does not justify omitting them or reducing their importance.

SHOULDERING THE BLAME

Customer contact employees are those who face customers, speak to customers, or write to customers. In this role, they represent the company or organization as much as does the product itself.

In this role of representing the company, often for a low wage and during undesirable hours, it is a primary service requirement that they possess the service skill of shouldering the blame for any problem the customer is experiencing. Yet this service skill is often missing from the job description.

While most companies will train a customer contact employee in what to do or what corrective action to take when a customer has a question, a problem, or a special request, more elementary generic service skills are necessary. These are the listening skill, to hear and understand what the customer is saying; the empathy skill, to feel with the customer his discomfort or annoyance; the verification skill that understands the problem or question and knows what will restore the customer's sense of satisfaction; and finally, the take-action skill, to remove the problem, answer the question, or fill the request.

These skills may be hard to define in a job description and harder still to evaluate during an interview or reference check, but they are essential. These abilities can make measurable repeat business gains for a company or organization.

JOB DESCRIPTIONS FOR OTHER EMPLOYEES

Job descriptions for other employees can be written similarly to those for customer contact employees. In a company or organization dominated by superior service goals, the job descriptions for these employees are likely to have many of the same elements as those for customer contact employees, as in the following examples:

1. To process receivables so that customers receive their bills on a timely basis.

2. To handle collections so that customers pay outstanding bills and still want to use this company again.

3. To make each hamburger so that customers enjoy it and want to purchase another.

4. To clean and make up the assigned hotel rooms so that guests feel comfortable and will want to stay in this hotel again.

5. To direct the marketing department so that profitable programs and products are placed in the hands of the sales force and so that these programs and products cause customers to use this company's product or service again and again.

6. To analyze and program a software system to specifications so that customers will receive the specified benefit and want to use this company's product or service again and again.

Each of these examples uses the word *customer* to describe why the job is important to the company. In superior service companies, all jobs in the organization are tied to the delivery of service to customers. In many, employees are viewed as either those who directly serve customers or those who work to support the customer contact staff.

PROFILES OF SUCCESSFUL PERFORMERS

Many people find it easier to state why the job exists and to enumerate its duties than to specify the skills needed, particularly the service skills.

One method for making this task easier is to look at the skills possessed by successful performers who are already doing the job and all its aspects well. A large enough sample needs to be taken, and the widest possible range of skills and attitudes needs to be considered.

The Avis manager in one state several years ago tried to make a profile of successful rental sales agents. His prime objective was to find a profile of rental sales agents who would stay with the company for several years. The only common criterion he could find was that his loyal and best performers were all divorced women. For a while, this manager hired only divorced women, yet his high turnover continued. One day he happened to read an article in a local magazine describing the turnover problems that many companies in the area were having as young people and divorced women migrated to the West Coast and stopped in this state to earn money to continue their journey. The manager's focus failed to get at the real criteria or characteristics which would guarantee loyalty and good performance.

Managers and executives do hear compliments about employees, such as, "John's very good with customers," or "Jane really knows how to handle customers." Carefully defining the behavior and attitudes of such employees helps identify selective factors for hiring new employees. Management should talk to these service-oriented employees, noting their reactions to questions and situations. Or human resource development, internal or external, may be used to develop a profile of the service skills and attitudes to look for in new employees.

As in any hiring exercise, it is important to know exactly what constitutes the job and exactly what skills, both technical and service, new employees should have. While the high turnover associated with front-line service employees is costly, it does provide an immediate opportunity to quickly hire the right people into the organization.

The most difficult part of turning a mediocre, poor, or inconsistent service company into a superior service company is not thinking of an idea. The most difficult part is the implementation of an idea. Involvement and commitment have to come from each and every member of the team.

One of the most useful ideas to get involvement of all team members is to involve front-line service employees in the development of a job description. To replace a gift shop employee, the three remaining employees can help construct the job description and list of required skills. These people are most familiar with the job's duties and required skills. The involvement and contributions of employees can be extremely significant.

SERVICE SKILLS AND ATTITUDES

A company that wants service excellence can make service easier to deliver. Having enough staff to serve customers, even during peak periods, is one way. Giving employees the necessary tools, training, and power to serve customers also helps. But these investments become even more powerful in terms of service delivery and gaining repeat business if the individual service delivery employees possess the correct service skills and attitudes.

To illustrate, consider a small department store having the policy of immediate refund on returned items. This policy is advertised locally and new staff members are trained in the procedures to follow, including asking customers to complete a short questionnaire about why they're returning the item. The store has an investment here—in training staff, in bearing the cost of the refund, in advertising, and in producing and analyzing the questionnaire. The expected result is that dissatisfied customers will be encouraged to claim the refund and shop in the store again, telling their friends about the experience, and that new and satisfied customers will shop in the store based on the confidence that any problems they have will be solved. While this is recognized as a sound service philosophy, it may prove to be a risky one, depending on how the message is conveyed by the employees. A customer returning an item might be greeted by an employee whose facial expressions, body language, tone of voice, and choice of words convey that the refund is cheerfully and willingly given. Or a customer returning an item might be greeted by an employee whose facial expressions, body language, tone of voice, and choice of words convey that the customer is a nuisance, that the refund is just store policy and causes the employee extra work, and even that the customer is doing something wrong by returning the item. In this case, the investment might produce no return for the store.

Good training can protect the store's investment. Salary, incentives, opportunity for promotion, quality assurance checks coupled with rewards and recognition, and good management techniques can play a vital role in protecting the investment. But hiring the right people who already possess the service skills and attitudes desired by the store is the best foundation for success.

Service skills and attitudes vary from job to job and from industry to industry. All service skills, however, are based on two key items: what customers expect and what the company's or organization's service strategy is.

If one is employing a pizza delivery person and the company has a service strategy of speedy delivery, the desirable employee is a person who always seems to be moving very fast. If one is employing a receptionist for a funeral parlor and the service strategy is one of sympathetic personal care, the desirable employee is a person who seems to take time to deal with each customer or who seems slow and relaxed.

Just as market research discovers what customers expect of a product or might need in a new product, so can it be used to find out what customers expect of service or might need in a new service. This research needs to encompass not just the service delivery aspects such as speed of delivery or refund policy but also the service skills and attitudes of the service delivery personnel. This research, coupled with the company's or organization's service strategy, can provide specific guidelines for such attributes as tone of voice (quiet and respectful for a funeral parlor, bright and cheerful for an amusement park, but never irritated); facial expression (serious and attentive in a hospital); body language and speed of motion (careful and measured in a barber shop); tact and level of patience; and others as they apply in specific jobs or industries.

Harder to ascertain during the hiring process are more general service skills and attitudes such as genuine concern for customers and people in general and the conceptual skills of understanding how the individual himself relates to the total organization or process.

RECRUITMENT MESSAGES

To work at Disney World, an applicant looks for the casting department rather than the personnel department and auditions for a

Role, rather than applies for the job, of putting on the daily Show for the Guests. Disney World sends a strong message to prospective job applicants on what its jobs are about and the skills and attitudes needed to do them.

Indeed, some companies and some industries already sit in a position of high appeal to service delivery personnel. Many young men and women want to work for airlines as flight attendants because of the travel benefits, even if the first two or three years find them flying short, crowded shuttle routes. When the Klosterbraeu Hotel interviews staff for the summer or winter season, many of Austria's brightest hotel school students are already in line for these coveted service delivery and service support positions.

While many other factors go into attracting the right personnel —such as a company's reputation for promoting from within, for good pay, for good working hours, for good benefits, and so forth —it is important to deliver a recruitment message that spells out the kind of job and the skills necessary to do it. To deliver superior service, the recruitment message must include this critical fact and ask for applicants who have experience or skills in service delivery, in satisfying customers' needs, and in turning an angry or confused customer into a happy one.

Whether using an employment agency, a newspaper ad, existing employees' recommendations, or word-of-mouth advertising to get applicants, the written or verbal message should be structured to say loudly and clearly that the company is looking for people to help deliver superior service.

INTERVIEWING

For a service delivery or customer contact position, the interview is a crucial step. The interviewer first meets a prospective job applicant similarly to the way customers will first meet this new employee. The foremost question in the interviewer's mind should be, "What will customers think of this person as a representative of the company?"

In 1969, Laura visited the offices of a newly established

company, Computer Auto-Match in Syracuse, New York, to apply for a job. She completed an application form and was then shown into the manager's office for an interview. He greeted her, placed his telephone near her, and walked out of the office. A few seconds later, the telephone rang and Laura decided to answer it. On the other end was the manager, who conducted the interview by telephone. The manager then returned to his office to advise Laura politely that the job depended totally on persuasive telephone selling and that she had failed to project this skill over the telephone.

Since customer contact employees may have contact with customers in person, by telephone, in writing, or by a combination of these methods, it seems logical that the interview should test the particular skills that will be used on the job. While Laura's story may sound rather brutal, it shows a time-efficient method of evaluating a skill critical to good performance of the job. A good photographer has a good eye for photogenic qualities in a model but also photographs the models and makes selections based on the results.

Interviewing must also test the skills that will be used on the job. If the prospective employee will deal with customers by telephone, the interview should include a test of how the employee sounds over the telephone. If the prospective employee will deal with customers by written correspondence, this skill must be tested.

Although many jobs will require training in company-specific technical details, much can be learned in the interview from "what if" questions. A "what if" question is simply one that poses a job situation and asks what the prospective employee might do in the situation. "What if" questions are like open-ended questions—they allow the applicant to speak (or to write or to speak via telephone) so that the interviewer can listen and evaluate what is being said and how.

There is also no harm in asking direct questions, such as how the applicant feels about customers and about serving customers. These kinds of questions deliver a strong message to the applicant about the company's commitment to the way its customers are handled.

REFERENCE CHECKING

Many service-oriented companies ask for references from previous employers and actually check these references. Checking often discovers only basic personnel records: length of service, salary, sick days taken, attendance, and so on.

Many companies do not have a way of classifying and assessing service performance—the level of customer satisfaction delivered by an employee to customers. And if a company does have some kind of employee service delivery rating, chances are it is not an industry or universal standard that can be understood without explanation.

Reference checking is, of course, important. The best situation is to reach the actual manager or supervisor closest to the employee and ask how effective the individual was in dealing with customers. This is often not possible or results in vague recollections. Still, employers should try it.

Some companies have reward and recognition schemes for individual employees or teams of employees. Include in reference checking a request about any reward and recognition schemes and what they mean, and for copies of complimentary or complaint letters received from customers about the employee. These bits of information about how the employee handled customers in previous jobs are as important as the routine facts about employment and attendance.

TESTING FOR SERVICE SKILLS AND ATTITUDES

Many service-oriented companies have devised pre-employment tests to evaluate service skills and attitudes. Designing such tests is not easy.

One test-design method is to employ an outside consultant to evaluate and recommend tests for applicants. Test questions need to be set against the service skills and attitudes needed for the job, again determined by the company's service strategy. Employing an external consultant necessitates defining the company's service strategy and the service skills and attitudes needed to do the job.

Other methods include using the human resources department and teams of high-performance employees to construct test questions.

Just as in interviewing, the most successful questions will include "what if" situations, asking the applicant to select from a series of alternatives in a service situation.

Service skills and attitudes often involve how the course of action is carried out, including such things as tone of voice, facial expression, and body language. Testing for service skills and attitudes must therefore also be done in the interview.

Professional psychological testing offers additional ways to determine team spirit and concern for other human beings.

PSYCHOLOGICAL EVALUATIONS

Many companies with strong service requirements have used psychological evaluations by trained psychologists to help select the right people to deliver service.

Such an expense is cost-justified against the cost of hiring, training, and inducting a new employee and the cost of losing repeat business because of service employees with the wrong attitudes.

The psychologist will need to know the company's service strategies and the desirable service skills and attitudes. While many companies can easily produce detailed statements of corporate objectives, goals, strategies, and plans, it is far harder to get a definition of the value systems that drive a company. For example, should a prospective employee have a strong competitive spirit or a strong spirit of teamwork, or a combination of both? Psychologists can provide detailed and useful analyses of prospective applicants only if the company can specify what it wants.

USING EMPLOYMENT AGENCIES

Recruitment time and effort can be saved by using employment agencies to screen and select the best candidates. However, the candidates selected by the employment agency will only be as good as the detailed person specifications and job descriptions given to the agency by the employer. Without research into and definition of precisely the type of person and skills desired the employment agency is unlikely to send the right applicants. On the other hand, a good employment agency armed with a precise definition of requirements can screen out unqualified applicants and save time by doing the reference checking.

Many employment agencies also offer assistance in designing and placing newspaper and trade magazine ads to attract the right applicants.

Some employment agencies derive their income from the job applicants and others derive their income from the employers. This focus may have an impact on the quality of the applicants passed to a company for consideration, but is less important than detailed person specifications and job descriptions.

SALARY AND BENEFITS

Salary and benefits are important factors in attracting service-oriented applicants. Yet many customer contact positions are paid at the lowest level with the least benefits.

Of course, most large organizations could not financially justify raising the salary levels and benefits of customer contact employees. Nor would such an action on its own create superior service. Writing in *Manager's Journal,* October 1987 (*Wall Street Journal*), Robert E. Kelley asserts that "high pay does not equal good service, and, as McDonald's has shown, low pay need not result in poor service."

If the company or organization wants to attract applicants with the best skills, salary and benefit offerings should be competitive—

with other companies in the same industry, with other companies looking for the same skills, and within the geographic location.

Because many customer contact positions are filled by young people just entering the work force, benefits may have powerful appeal. The airline industry is a prime example, allowing travel benefits that young people find attractive, yet imposing restrictions so that the benefit is not costly to the airline. While acting as a benefit, the travel privilege also allows employees to experience the product as a customer. With some imagination, most companies can construct benefits that applicants will find attractive and that allow employees to sample the product. These benefits may adequately supplement a relatively low salary base.

A second powerful appeal is the opportunity for rapid advancement and promotion that can outweigh the detraction of low salary and undesirable working hours.

PROBATIONARY PERIODS

Many companies use a period of probationary employment to enable both employer and employee to try out the new environment. A probationary period needs to be a test situation for both parties rather than a substitute for good interviewing and selection techniques by the employer. Care must be taken to involve the employee in the job and all of its aspects rather than using it as an excuse not to provide uniforms, training, or benefits.

GUIDELINES FOR CHIEF EXECUTIVES

Chief executives should be concerned with the company's ability to get the right people to deliver service. Customer contact employees face, talk to, and write to customers each day. Even if the chief executive's face appears in television commercials to attract new customers and build the company's image, it is the individual interactions that customer contact employees have with customers each day that produce satisfied or dissatisfied customers, repeat purchases or lost business.

Chief executives should consider whether in social contacts or business contacts with young people, they speak about the company's customer contact positions and encourage young people to apply for them. They should seize opportunities for themselves and other senior executives to speak at universities, business schools, and trade schools to attract bright young people to the company. They must take the time or send other senior executives to speak at conferences and meetings that might attract applicants.

As chief executives visit the company's service delivery points, they should observe the service being delivered to customers versus that of competitors and ask the line manager how he or she recruits new employees. They need to occasionally review turnover statistics and ask the management team how they go about getting the right people to deliver service.

Chief executives generally do not hire the customer contact employees themselves, but must be concerned with the skills of the people who represent the company to its customers.

GUIDELINES FOR FRONT-LINE SERVICE DELIVERY PERSONNEL

Front-line service delivery employees should consider themselves part of the company's advertising and recruitment message. Their ability to explain the job with realism and enthusiasm makes a powerful recruitment message for friends and acquaintances. Some companies actively solicit recommendations from employees for new employees and even reward successful referrals. Whether the company does this as policy, service delivery employees can refer prospective recruits with a sense of additional satisfaction that they are helping the company to get the right people to deliver service.

GUIDELINES FOR BACK-OFFICE SERVICE SUPPORT PERSONNEL

Back-office service support employees can also consider themselves part of the company's advertising and recruitment message. Their ability to explain the job with realism and enthusiasm makes a powerful recruitment message for friends and acquaintances. Some companies actively solicit recommendations from employees for new employees and even reward successful referrals. Whether the company has this policy, back-office personnel can refer new employees with a sense of additional satisfaction that they are helping the company get the right people for service support positions.

GUIDELINES FOR MIDDLE MANAGEMENT

Middle managers, in addition to other duties, most often do the actual hiring of new employees for front-line service delivery and back-office service support. Managers who participate in hiring should ask themselves the following:

1. Do I have an accurate job description for each position for which I must hire people?

2. Do I have an accurate person specification of the skills needed to do the job?

3. Am I using the most effective recruitment methods to attract the right applicants?

4. Do my interviews ask "what if" questions and allow the applicant to demonstrate his or her service skills and attitudes?

5. Do I use all of the available ways to assess applicants, such as reference checking, employment agencies, and psychological evaluation?

6. Am I able to explain attractively the salary and benefits?

7. Do I have sound criteria upon which to base my selection?

8. Do I actively seize any opportunities to speak to prospective applicants in social or business situations and encourage them to apply for jobs in my company or organization?

9. Do I keep in touch with competitive salary and benefit offerings and make justified recommendations for change when appropriate?

10. Do I assign the recruitment and selection process the right priority so that I am not simply hiring warm bodies?

4

Create an Organizational Structure That Fosters Service

In 1981, the advertising department of a major car rental company was charged with the task of developing new promotions to get more customers to rent cars. In isolation they developed some coupons for publication in major magazines. These coupons turned up at rental counters in the hands of customers, so the advertising department produced even more coupons, aided by enthusiastic interest from allied industries and travel clubs. Buoyed by this enthusiasm and the possibility of huge successes, they produced more and more coupons—each with a different name, each with different conditions of use, each with a fresh new look. In their haste to take maximum advantage of this opportunity, they put aside a growing barrage of telephone calls and memos from the training department and from rental stations asking how to handle the various coupons, certificates, vouchers, and so on.

The training department tried writing up handling procedures to be printed on the coupons themselves so that service delivery staff would need only to read the coupon to know how to handle it. But more frequently than not, the coupons went to print with no instructions or with incorrect instructions. In addition, the conditions of use for customers were often unclear, misleading, or incomplete.

The result was long lines of customers at rental counters waiting for their coupons, certificates, and vouchers to be deciphered by front-line service delivery personnel. Additional letters and phone calls flooded into the customer service department. Customers loved the coupons—until they had to wait for a long time at the rental counter to get a car. Service delivery personnel and their managers were delighted with the additional business—until it began taking them about 30 minutes to decipher and process each coupon. The end result was dissatisfied customers (including new ones encouraged to rent by the coupon offers) and dissatisfied staff.

ORIGINATION OF IDEAS

A company or organization with a commitment to service depends upon the continuous origination of ideas to get new customers, to satisfy existing customers and cause them to purchase again, and to cut costs. Somehow the ideas have to originate in all areas of the organization, and they have to pass through other areas of the organization to be effectively executed.

Ideas originate in the minds of geniuses, of ordinary human beings, and of those with only the simplest level of intelligence. Most organizations have found that ideas originate from people at all levels, whether or not they are solicited. The most common difficulty is finding the way from idea to effective execution. More often than not, an ineffectively executed idea becomes known as a bad idea or an idea that didn't work.

This places the burden on the originator of an idea to define its effective execution, that is, to define the idea in such detail that the success of its execution is guaranteed. When this becomes the rule, fewer ideas originate because not many people in the organization have the background in all functional areas to detail the execution. A freer structure is needed to allow ideas to pass through various functional areas toward successful execution.

Marketing often faces this problem. Successful marketers possess not just the creativity to originate ideas and the marketing disciplines to allow them to follow through; they must possess a buoyant, optimistic commitment to counter the rejection they face at each step. The accounting people say it won't work; the legal people say it's illegal or misleading; the sales people say it won't sell; the operations people say it won't work; manufacturing says it can't be made; and a variety of others say it's another one of those crazy marketing ideas that doesn't work.

The organizational structure must allow the origination of service ideas, including the refinement and definition of those ideas to their execution. The most successful method known has been development of a service strategy.

SERVICE STRATEGY

A service strategy is a brief statement that combines the results of market research or what customers want with the overall business goals and objectives as well as value system of a company. A service strategy gives a framework or point of reference for the origination of ideas in a service delivery environment. It also serves as a readily quoted goal toward which the company or organization is working.

A good service strategy contains an element of marketing: defining customer segments. Or it could be said that the service strategy is linked directly to the marketing effort. The Austrian government has had for many years a service strategy of creating a vacation paradise for tourists. As a result, the streets are cleaned between 4:00 A.M. and 5:00 A.M., and garbage trucks travel on separate roads in resort villages. Hotel and restaurant supply deliveries go through doors and travel on streets the average tourist never sees. All of these expensive activities are undertaken in the name of the service strategy: creating a vacation paradise for tourists where they are not reminded of the everyday activities of life back home.

The crucial point is that the Austrian government has communicated this service strategy effectively to most of the country's residents and work force. Thus, it is unlikely to find people suggesting cost savings by cleaning the streets between 9:00 A.M. and 5:00 P.M. or increasing hotel revenues by promoting heavy business conferences during the peak tourist season.

Excellent definitions of service strategy are contained in Karl Albrecht's and Ron Zemke's *Service America* (1985). They stress the importance of communicating the service strategy to all areas of the organization to provide a basis for the origination of appropriate ideas.

EXECUTION OF IDEAS

New ideas should be executed in a logical progression. Unfortunately, there is no model successful pattern, but rather many successful patterns.

Some companies are famous for employing competing teams to work on the origination and execution of similar, competitive, or even the same idea. Other companies use a formal approval structure with commitment to ensure that an idea is evaluated from all angles.

Whatever the pattern, some common factors usually appear:

1. More than one person can claim ownership of the idea. Said another way, many people "buy in" to the idea. We all must have examples of the implemented, successful idea, the procedure only to be discontinued when its originator leaves the company.

2. Many people can claim key participation in the execution of the idea and can therefore share satisfaction in its success. Often this participation may have been forced or bartered for, but after successful execution, people forget most negative feelings.

3. Measuring the success of an idea is not always done in hard, cold, factual profit and revenue figures, although these are important. Unmeasured customer satisfaction, improved employee morale, and better quality are often considered success. Numbers are often manipulated to suit the user, and thus sometimes the more subjective judgments rule.

4. The organization will allow change for the better but not change for the worse and usually not change for its own sake. This sounds quite logical, but there are many examples of organizations that resist change, either as a timely or long-term strategy. There are also many examples of organizations that change for the sake of change—a fresh new look, fresh new product ideas with no research, new personnel. The most successful approach is change for the better.

Execution of ideas, because it usually involves many people in the organization, is most difficult, but many companies have shown it is not impossible.

INVERTED PYRAMID STRUCTURE

Jan Carlzon, President of Scandinavian Airlines System (SAS), took over an ailing airline with six owners, including three governments, and turned it into a profitable airline favored by business travelers. A cornerstone in his success story is the inverted pyramid structure he introduced to turn the organization upside down and put the decisionmaking power into the hands of SAS employees, who dealt with each "moment of truth" or customer contact.

The principle is simple to understand; it means listening to the employees who have daily contact with customers to find out what kind of service customers want. But only a brave and bold management truly inverts the organizational chart and allows the frontline service delivery personnel to make decisions.

In any organization, the inverted pyramid approach to service delivery can supplement expensive market research and customer surveys. It places power in the hands of service delivery personnel to select a course of action to satisfy customers. Rather than spending money to develop and train detailed procedures for every conceivable customer situation, it encourages employees to think and exercise judgment within the framework of the company's service strategy.

Contrary to what a company controller might think, the experience at SAS and other companies demonstrates that employees with this freedom do not "give away the store." Rather, they feel responsible for company profits because of the faith placed in them.

A sales organization made an experiment in human performance dynamics. They selected 20 average sales representatives, called 10 together and told them that while their performance had been satisfactory until now, the company had much higher standards for the future and would not be able to keep them unless they improved. They called together the other 10 and told them they had been selected for a super team of sales representatives with high potential. Both groups were given the same targets of numbers of sales to be made. The group who believed their jobs were on the line performed below the targets, with some of the group resigning to find other jobs. The group that believed they had been selected for a super team surpassed the targets and, in fact, became a super team of sales representatives for the organization.

QUALITY CIRCLES

Another successful organizational approach that fosters service and generates ideas for successful execution is the use of quality circles. Quality circles provide an organized method to originate and execute ideas for quality and service improvement. Julia Morland, writing for the Industrial Society (1981), provides a simple definition of quality circles.

Small groups of employees, usually from the same workplace and under the same supervisor or leading hand, volunteer to meet for problem spotting and solving sessions. They look at problems that occur in their work area and that affect their own job. The group itself applies the solutions if they have the authority. Otherwise management is presented with their recommendations, and implementation then rests with management.

As with any new approach, it is best to learn all of the successes and pitfalls experienced by other companies and organizations. Quality circles fail to produce the desired results when implemented in haste without training for all participants to understand the process, when constructed incorrectly without management representation or with too many participants, and when participants are not empowered to develop and define the execution of their ideas. Quality circles, like many other approaches, require long-term commitment to ensure that they are not a "flavor of the month" or this spring's bright idea. They function best as an ongoing organizational activity that must be learned and practiced by many within the organization to obtain maximum results.

JOB ROTATION

At almost any company or organization are at least a few persons who would say, "*They* don't understand my job." Whether it is line staff saying that headquarters staff do not understand, back-office service support staff saying front-line service delivery personnel do not understand, manufacturing personnel saying sales personnel do not understand, or any variation on these patterns, every company or organization seems doomed to face the accusation that employees do not fully understand what other employees in the organization do.

British Airways felt so strongly about this facet that they instituted a training program called "A Day in the Life of . . ." which helped employees understand how the various roles fit together to produce satisfied customers. Other companies make similar but less extensive attempts during initial training to acquaint new employees with the various roles and their interrelationships.

Another successful approach is job rotation. Job rotation means more than spending a day or week in another person's job. Job rotation is an organizational activity that allows employees to move to other disciplines within the company in order to strengthen their skill base.

A simple form of job rotation is a management trainee program where university graduates are recruited and put through an accelerated and carefully monitored program of job placements to learn the business. A management trainee program might ask the trainee to perform in each of eight different jobs for a period of 12 weeks each over the course of two years, ending in a supervisory or management position.

More sophisticated job rotation programs include those used as requirements for promotion. For example, experience over the course of three to five years in several front-line service delivery positions may be required before an employee may be considered for the job of customer service representative in the customer service department. Job rotation can also include doing the same job in a different geographic location.

Often job rotation is associated with a manufacturing or rote activity. However, many service companies and organizations use it as a way of strengthening the pool of potential middle managers and of relieving the pressure in certain intense job environments.

Job rotation is best undertaken with the commitment and involvement of the human resources department so that salary, benefits, and rewards remain commensurate with the additional skills acquired by rotating employees. Also, rotating employees may require guaranteed career counseling from a human resources department as they move from discipline to discipline, losing contact with a mentor.

JOB ENGINEERING

Job engineering means altering or engineering the job descriptions to fit the skills and attitudes of current employees. It is not a one-time adjustment but rather a continuing organizational activity designed to make maximum use of the company's human resources.

In the service industry, job engineering can be extremely useful as an organization moves from service orientation to service obsession. Since no one formula has proved particularly or exclusively successful, jobs can be restructured creatively to achieve the service strategy. Rather than leap into the commitment of a full-time person to look after a specific new service need, the skills of several existing employees may be used to carry out the tasks and thereby define the need.

Job engineering also includes using employees on medium-range projects outside the scope of their existing jobs. During its two-year project to implement the Wizard computer system at over two hundred locations in 13 European countries, the Avis training department used a development team at head office that included permanent training personnel plus training personnel seconded for eight-month periods from the countries involved. Rather than selecting country personnel with specified skills, jobs and tasks were engineered to fit the skills of the persons selected by the countries. In addition, as each country carried out the training activity just prior to implementation, front-line service delivery personnel were seconded to the country training department to carry out the training. Again, their tasks were assigned to fit the skills each brought to the assignment. Most of the employees who participated in these assignments were subsequently promoted back in their own job environment.

Job engineering usually requires the commitment and involvement of the human resources department, which may be required to provide creative solutions to job engineering maneuvers that combine the duties and skills of several jobs at varying pay scales.

VISIBLE MANAGEMENT

Visible management is a technique used by many companies to keep senior management, middle management, and back-office personnel in contact with customers. At Disney World, senior executives spend several days each year performing routine service delivery jobs such as taking tickets or selling hot dogs. This activity also demonstrates to all employees the commitment of senior management to superior service delivery.

To the manager facing a visible management experience, the idea is often, of course, good—but frightening. The experience may require preparation—learning complex procedures and new techniques. And usually, the manager must work next to employees who perform the job each day—and are just waiting to see how the manager performs. To the manager who can prepare a bit and overcome the humiliation and possible embarrassment, the rewards are great. There is almost always instant rapport with customers who are happy to divulge their opinions on all aspects of service. There is almost always rapport and communication with service delivery personnel who are also happy to divulge their opinions on procedures and service improvement. The experience usually results in a positive feeling about the company's service strategy and what can be done to make improvements.

The pitfalls include a false confidence that visible management has provided all the answers. Market research, customer satisfaction surveys, quality circle input, and so forth, also continue to be important sources of information. Another mistake is to carry out the visible management experience as a simple field visit—chatting and having a cup of coffee with customers and employees. The service delivery job must be felt and experienced—with the same pressure and intensity and hours as a typical service delivery employee experiences.

MANAGEMENT BY WALKING ABOUT

Management by walking about is simply a process whereby managers visit service delivery locations. It may be called field visits or management by walking the shop floor. Managers in the manufacturing process used to walk the shop floor to make spot checks on the quality of the product being manufactured and to talk to shop workers. In today's service environment managers visit service delivery points to make spot checks on the quality of service being delivered and to talk to employees.

The objectives of this process include ordinary service delivery employees (and also service support employees) being able to see and talk to members of the management team whom they do not normally see, as well as the obvious benefits of keeping management in touch with day-to-day decisions they may have to make about capital expenditures, office renovation, customer needs in specific locations, salary or recruitment difficulties, and the like. In addition, this method allows management to observe a limited amount of first-hand service delivery.

If managers walk about or make field visits, they should pay close attention to everything happening at the points of service delivery. Employees should not have to fear termination or punishment from such visits. But management should question service delivery and why procedures and actions are being used.

CONCEPTUAL SKILLS

In most corporations, much effort is devoted to developing technical skills. Also, many corporations have devoted effort to developing the behavioral skills of all levels of supervisory and management employees.

In the service industry, however, the critical skills for tomorrow's success are conceptual skills—the ability to see how one's activities relate to the ever-changing overall goals, objectives, and service strategies of the company or organization and to intuitively make decisions and take actions that enhance these goals. Conceptual skills are needed at all levels, particularly by frontline service delivery personnel, back-office service support personnel, and their managers.

Conceptual skills can be improved through formal training and development activities, or by the actual organizational structure and management style.

Conversely, the organizational structure can discourage development of these skills. For example, Lufthansa Airlines has a formal organizational structure within which a service delivery employee is many reporting levels away from the top of the organization. Lufthansa uses extensive market research and consumer studies to construct its service strategy, which is then translated into detailed procedures. Employees receive thorough and comprehensive training in these procedures. The result is a thoroughly mechanized or robotized delivery of precision service. "Warm" and "caring" are not words generally associated with it. The ability to exercise and use conceptual skills in this setting is restricted. Little judgment is needed; a rule or procedure covers every situation. This approach is in direct contrast to the inverted pyramid structure used by SAS.

Conceptual skills can be developed in job rotation and by job engineering as well as by an organizational structure that is not rigid and allows communication between all levels of employees.

POWER GROUPS

One day, Patty, a newly recruited member of the training department, became interested in the organizational structure of her company. She took the organization directory and counted fifty-eight vice presidents (or higher) worldwide. All were male and white. Surprised, she took this information to her boss, who, of course, asked her why she didn't get busy with her assigned work.

The official, and unofficial, organizational charts and directories of companies and organizations tell a powerful story that sometimes varies from stated or published strategies. Most people have at one time or another believed that "accountants run the company" or that "marketing people always have their own way" or that "the legal people tie our hands in making significant progress."

In *Director* magazine (November 1987), Richard Davis, training manager for Avis in the United Kingdom, describes the success of Avis's quality of service in the United Kingdom in terms of the emergence of two power groups: finance and marketing; and operations, personnel, and training. Davis says that the organizational structure is shallow and that each of the functional heads of finance, marketing, operations, personnel, and training "report to the Managing Director on an equal and distinct footing."

There is no doubt that power groups—or more specifically the emergence of one power group over all others—have an impact on the service that customers experience. In a company committed to superior service delivery, a balance must exist among the power groups so that each decision results in customer satisfaction *and* profit for the company or organization, and satisfaction and profit must have equal weight. Too often making a profit takes priority because it is expressed in tangible numeric terms. But customer satisfaction can also be expressed numerically using the formulas established by Technical Assistance Research Programs, Inc. (TARP).

PROMOTIONS

The opportunity for promotion and advancement has broad organizational power. In service industries where entry-level positions offer low salary and benefits, the potential for promotion and advancement prompts outstanding performance. McDonald's is a good example. Also, Avis in many countries has long recognized the importance of the front-line management position of its station managers. Yet these positions offer a low salary, attracting by benefits (driving a rental car home each day) and rapid advancement (from rental sales agent to station manager, from a small station to a larger station, from station manager to district manager).

Whether or not promotions are official structured events, the feeling of movement and advancement needs to exist in the minds of employees. There is also a small effect on customers from this upward movement. At Pizza Hut, for example, name badges reflect titles earned for outstanding service and completion of advanced training. Customers watching a favorite waitress or waiter earning new titles feel they have somehow participated in the success. On the other hand, care must be taken to ensure personalized service continues to repeat customers who may resent that their usual service delivery person—who knew all of their special requirements and needs—has been promoted and moved to a new location. The Hotel Europa in Innsbruck, Austria, overcomes this risk by keeping house cards on repeat guests.

JOB ENRICHMENT

Another organizational tool that fosters service is job enrichment: adding tasks, duties, and responsibilities to existing jobs or finding more interesting ways to perform existing jobs. Probably the most famous job enrichment activity was the experiment many years ago by Volvo in Sweden to use teams to assemble units of cars so that some of the boredom of assembly-line work was relieved and productivity improved.

Job enrichment sometimes requires a company to undertake training and development to raise the skill levels of employees. Writing in *Manager's Journal,* October 1987 (*Wall Street Journal*), Robert E. Kelley describes the education programs, pictorial color-coded instructional material, and performance-based promotion opportunities by ServiceMaster Company to overcome high employee illiteracy. "The results: low turnover in these traditionally high-turnover jobs; productivity levels higher than industry averages; and an average of 30% return on equity after taxes from 1973 to 1985."

Job enrichment can be less formal than this, done by simply throwing out some of the heavy procedures and rule books and asking employees to devise their own styles within the service strategy.

GUIDELINES FOR CHIEF EXECUTIVES

Chief executives have enormous power as well as enormous constraints. But it is unlikely that even chief executives can take out a blank sheet of paper and create the organization and power structure they would like to have. Far more often the task is to change what exists. And that takes time, money, effort, commitment, and strength as shareholders, governments, the general public, and new owners snap at their heels.

Whatever the approach, chief executives need to ask themselves:

1. Do ideas originate and get executed, both successfully and unsuccessfully, in my company?

2. Does my company have a service strategy and do employees at all levels know it?

3. How many days have I spent in the last year actually working as a customer contact employee in my company?

4. How many hours have I spent in the last year actually visiting the points where service delivery and service support activities take place and speaking with employees?

5. Do my company's organizational structure and approaches promote the development of conceptual skills in employees at all levels?

6. Do I balance customer satisfaction and company profits equally?

GUIDELINES FOR FRONT-LINE SERVICE DELIVERY PERSONNEL

People who work in front-line service delivery positions often feel they have no power to influence organization structure. Reading about the inverted pyramid structure at SAS or the assembly teams at Volvo may create dreams of some day working for a company that recognizes their vital role.

But most organizations undergo continuous change because they are made up of people who come and go, people who learn new skills, people who change positions. Organizational change may not happen as fast as one wishes, but it does happen, and employees should prepare to change in response.

Front-line service delivery personnel need to ask themselves:

1. Do I know what my company's service strategy is? If there isn't an openly stated or published strategy, can I surmise what it is from the decisions and policies I can observe?

2. How often do I contribute ideas for service improvement through the channels available to me?

3. When I contribute ideas, do I use all sources of information available to me to make the idea as realistic to execute as possible?

4. Do I actively volunteer for projects, assignments, and positions that will allow me to contribute and help me develop new skills?

5. Do I encourage colleagues to do the same?

6. For each decision I make or each customer contact I have, do I try to consider how it fits with the company's overall goals, directions, and service strategy?

Front-line service delivery personnel owe it to themselves to consider these questions and to take seriously their sometimes limited but always vital role in helping the organization to grow in the right direction.

GUIDELINES FOR BACK-OFFICE SERVICE SUPPORT PERSONNEL

People who work in back-office service support positions often feel they have no power to influence organizational structure. They may even feel that if change happens, the front-line service delivery personnel will be the first to benefit from greater recognition and participation in it.

But superior service delivery is dependent upon both sides: those who deliver service directly to customers and those who perform the support functions that allow good service to be delivered.

Satisfying customers means that both groups have to work toward the same goals. Changes in service delivery and customer satisfaction almost always involve both groups of employees.

Back-office service support personnel need to ask themselves:

1. Do I know what my company's service strategy is? If there isn't an openly stated or published strategy, can I surmise what it is from the decisions and policies I can observe?

2. How often do I contribute ideas for service improvement through the channels available to me?

3. When I contribute ideas, do I use all sources of information available to me to make the idea as realistic to execute as possible?

4. Do I actively volunteer for projects, assignments, and positions that will allow me to contribute and help me develop new skills?

5. Do I encourage colleagues to do the same?

6. For each decision I make or each job duty I carry out, do I try to consider how it fits with the company's overall goals, directions, and service strategy?

Back-office service support personnel must consider these questions and take seriously their sometimes limited but always vital role in helping the organization to grow in the right direction.

GUIDELINES FOR MIDDLE MANAGEMENT

For middle managers organizational structure is often a crucial issue. They may have just moved up from being "at the bottom," or in various stages of working toward being "at the top." Individually, middle managers often say they can do nothing to create an organizational structure that fosters service. But organizational change happens most often in middle management, and collectively, these managers possess enormous power to initiate and execute organizational change.

Within their own areas of responsibility middle managers have the power to test and implement ideas for service improvement and for organizational change. They also have the power to create job rotation and job engineering in collaboration with colleagues. They hold the power to progress the ideas of subordinates, and the power to translate executive orders into inspirational directions. But managers also carry the responsibility and accountability for keeping themselves in touch with customers, employees, and service delivery and for bringing out the best skills and attitudes in staff.

5

Train and Develop People to Deliver Service

Marie, an American living and working in London, put in a busy day at the office and took the evening flight to New York. Arriving late at Kennedy Airport, she found the bank closed, but she rented a car and drove to the New York Hilton. She had just enough American money to tip the porter who carried her baggage to her room. It felt wonderful to return to America, even for a business trip. After a good night's sleep, Marie awoke with a homesick hunger for an American breakfast. She dialed room service.

"Good morning, room service," answered a sunny voice after only one ring.

Marie gave the sunny voice a healthy order. The voice responded to Marie using Marie's name and room number, visible on a computer screen in the room service department, and assured Marie that her large American breakfast would be delivered in 20 minutes.

Exactly 20 minutes later, a smiling waiter wheeled in a table and made a great show of opening the flaps, positioning the table so that Marie could look out the window as she ate, laying out the silverware, and so forth. His penultimate action was to open a heated compartment underneath the table and set out a steaming hot plate of American breakfast. It was just what Marie wanted!

The waiter then handed Marie the bill. She quickly added a generous tip and signed her name, eager to dive into the hot meal.

"I'm sorry, but you have to pay cash," said the waiter.

"But I don't have any American money yet; can't I just sign this to my room?" asked Marie, watching the food begin to cool.

The waiter mumbled something about having to check in with a major credit card, which only prompted Marie to open her wallet full of credit cards, displaying the American Express gold card that she had presented when checking in. Reluctantly, the waiter shuffled to the telephone. Five minutes of discussion and waiting produced the answer that she could charge the breakfast to her room.

The waiter left. Marie sat down to a cold breakfast.

TRAINING FOR CUSTOMER SATISFACTION

All training must result in customer satisfaction. The New York Hilton has a significant investment in a computer system that allows the room service department to address a guest by name. They have an investment in heated compartments to keep food hot while it is being transported to guests' rooms. They have an investment in training staff to answer the phone and take orders correctly, in training staff to set out a meal in a room for the guest's enjoyment. But, in Marie's case, all of this investment only produced a dissatisfied customer.

Whether there is a missing investment in a computer system that conveys guests' credit card information to the room service computer, a missing investment in devising and training a procedure to settle the bill before removing the hot food from the heated compartment (or the encouragement of conceptual skills that would cause waiters to figure this out themselves), or a disciplinary problem with waiters pocketing cash while charging a meal to another guest's room, the end result is a dissatisfied customer.

Technical skills training and some behavioral skills training are based on agreed upon procedures and policies shaped by the company's service strategy. Whether these policies and procedures are developed by the service staff themselves, by a methods and procedures department, by management, or by the training department, training is based on these policies and procedures. Delivering a training program cannot proceed when procedures are not agreed upon, don't exist, or are so weak that they inevitably result in customer dissatisfaction.

Companies cannot leave customer satisfaction to chance. Customer satisfaction is a delicately approached goal that must be carefully defined and trained. Companies with a commitment to superior service must train and develop their employees to deliver superior service. And that training must be given to all groups of employees at all levels so that the groups perform at maximum capability toward the overall goal and service strategy.

TECHNICAL SKILLS TRAINING

Almost all service delivery and service support positions require some technical skills training that enables the employee to perform the job in the manner desired by the company. Sometimes technical skills are a requirement for hiring, such as legal qualifications for a legal assistant, typing and shorthand skills for a secretary, selling skills for a sales representative. But the company may wish to train specific applications of these technical skills that fit the company's own service strategy.

Technical skills training is given to new employees to enable them to do the job. Technical skills training may also be required when jobs change, when employees are promoted or rotated to another job, or when new skills are required in support of new products, new procedures, or new computer systems.

Training can be defined simply as an activity that produces a change in behavior. Good training depends on analysis of the existing skills and needed skills. The gap between the two forms the objectives of training. Objectives are stated in behavioral terms, telling what the employee will be able to do at the end of the training period. They serve as a contract between student and instructor.

Training begins by knowing the behaviors and actions that produce satisfied customers. Training is an activity that can never be done in isolation. It depends upon the interrelation of many functions: a definition of customer needs from marketing, a framework of policies and procedures from accounting and administration, standards of performance from the quality area, and so forth.

Confidence in dealing with customers comes from knowledge. Technical skills training gives customer contact employees the knowledge to deal with customers confidently. Customer contact employees experience intense frustration facing a customer and not having the answers.

For this reason, most good service companies do not allow new employees to serve customers before they have been trained. Training employees before they serve customers is cost-effective, reduces turnover, prevents costly errors, and eliminates possible causes of customer dissatisfaction. Some companies have put new employees to work serving customers to try them out or let them "get the feel of it" before investing money in training them. This produces high turnover as new employees feel frustrated in front of customers, and it exposes the company to errors and lost customers. Fortunately the medical profession does not allow would-be surgeons to operate on patients before extensive training. A company's customers are the lifeblood of its business, and allowing untrained new employees to serve customers can be just as life threatening.

BEHAVIORAL SKILLS TRAINING

Behavioral skills training is a term that describes a broad range of supervisory and management skills training programs in, for example, delegating, interviewing, controlling, leading, motivating, and planning. Because both technical skills and behavioral skills training rely on a change in behavior against specified objectives, they are somewhat similar. The primary difference is that behavioral skills involve tasks for which there is seldom a distinct beginning and end (i.e., they are continuous activities) and for which there is no specific correct procedure (i.e., many approaches work and many do not). For this reason, many training programs referred to as customer contact training or customer service training have been categorized as behavioral skills training.

Behavioral skills training for new employees is often overlooked or is treated as tacked on to the technical skills training program. To produce customer satisfaction, the most successful approaches merge the two so that new employees do not perceive a difference.

In a skillful combination of technical and behavioral skills training, Swissair's new employees receive much of their technical skills training at their home base with programmed learning materials before they fly to the sophisticated Swissair training center in Zurich to learn how to serve customers.

Some companies give new employees technical skills training during their initial employment and then bring them back to the classroom for customer contact training 6 or 12 months later. Good service delivery that meets customer expectations depends on a combination of technical skills and behavioral skills.

While both technical skills training and behavioral skills training can produce a change in behavior according to the instructional objectives (for further reading, see Mager, Robert F., *Preparing Instructional Objectives*, Palo Alto, California: Fearon Publishers 1962), management often expects customer contact training to change attitudes as well. This produces a real challenge to a training effort that has become comfortable with demonstrable behavioral change as fathered by Robert F. Mager.

Amy Titus, speaking at the IFTDO World Conference in Madrid in July 1987, suggested that trainers need to move beyond Mager's performance-based objectives to training that takes on attitude change. In fact, the success of the "Putting People First" training at British Airways and similar customer contact training programs undertaken by Time Manager International is attributed to attitude change, and these programs are sold to companies on the basis of attitude change.

Many trainers may argue that attitude change subsequently generates a change in behavior and thus there is nothing new in these approaches. Whether there is newness or not, every possible approach needs to be considered. Whatever approach works is certainly right, regardless of what name is assigned to it.

TRAINING VERSUS ON-THE-JOB PERFORMANCE

Whatever training is done, both technical and behavioral skills must be demonstrated as on-the-job performance that produces customer satisfaction. The training department should not operate in isolation, but rather teach job skills that can be and are applied.

At Avis, newly hired rental sales agents were trained to handle customers returning cars. They learned to ask customers for the keys to the car (otherwise, Avis might have to cut a new set), they learned to ask customers if the car was satisfactory (so that any faults could be investigated or repaired), and they learned to ask customers if they would like a reservation for their next Avis rental (a selling technique to get customers committed to Avis). Performance was demonstrated and checked during role plays in the classroom. Back on the job at some stations, new employees were quickly "clued in" by long-serving employees that they didn't have to ask customers if they would like a reservation for their next Avis rental. After all, Avis had a toll-free reservation number. At other stations, new employees were told by their managers, "When it's really busy, just make sure you get the keys, because it costs us money to cut new keys."

Service delivery principles and procedures should be agreed upon, trained, reinforced on the job, and audited, in the same ways as are accounting and administrative procedures. Sometimes this includes training management or reviewing new service delivery principles and procedures with management before employees are trained. Other training programs such as management and sales courses may need to be altered to include the financial benefits of customer satisfaction—and the market damage of customer dissatisfaction—as well as the service delivery principles that support it.

A common error is to train only isolated skills, even though this approach appears to be cost-effective. A new computer system or major hardware or software alterations to the system used by service delivery employees may be taught this way. It seems cost-effective to train the computer skills using computer-based instruction or computer-assisted instruction, especially if the existing system is being altered. But service delivery skills and customer contact skills, if not included in training, will deteriorate, as employees concentrate on operating the computer system. Service delivery procedures may need revision to fit the computer system.

ADULT TRAINING TECHNIQUES

Even though many service delivery jobs are often taken up by young people not long away from school, the use of adult training techniques may produce optimum results, particularly in behavioral skills and attitude.

Adults take pride in what they have already learned and the skills they already possess. Training techniques must build on this knowledge, allowing adults to contribute what they already know to the learning process. Standard lecture techniques, including presentations on why it's important to be nice to customers, often give adults the feeling that they are being talked down to.

New employees generally welcome training that enables them to perform their new jobs. Existing employees, however, often approach customer contact training with some of the following attitudes:

"We already know how to do our jobs properly."

"Why do we need more training?"

"What can the training department teach us?"

"We'll just learn a bunch of time-consuming procedures that can't be applied on the job."

"Our manager has very strong views about how things should be done, so I doubt we'll be allowed to use anything we learn."

"Our customers are different at our location, and we know what's best for them."

These types of attitudes may face trainers and make them feel that students are hostile. To combat hostility the trainer can begin the course for existing employees with a review of technical procedures and skills, allowing students to realize for themselves (and not for public embarrassment) that they may not know everything. Another successful technique is to allow employees to assist in shaping the course objectives, a technique that requires great adaptability in the trainer.

The most successful adult learning techniques are those that allow maximum student participation. Not only are adults proud but they feel best when they believe they are helping to shape their destiny and making a contribution. Challenging case studies, realistic role plays, analyses of competitors' services, and enthusiastic discussions are better received than lectures, programmed learning, and rote exercises.

Customer contact trainers should follow some of the same guidelines that make other training programs successful, such as training or reviewing the training materials with students' managers before presentation, producing course announcements that generate enthusiasm, selecting desirable sites for the courses, and arranging the classroom to encourage maximum participation.

USING ROLE PLAYS

Role plays are a training technique frequently used to combine technical and behavioral skills training for service delivery positions, whether the employees are new or experienced. Role plays allow demonstration of skills possessed and skills learned during training. Role plays may be constructed as face-to-face customer transactions, as telephone transactions, as written transactions, or as a combination, depending on how the employees communicate with customers. Face-to-face role play transactions may be videotaped for playback and analysis or to allow the role play to take place in a separate room from the classroom. Telephone transactions may be audiotaped for playback and analysis or to allow the role play to take place in a separate room. Written transactions can easily be photocopied or made into overhead visuals for group analysis and feedback.

Like other training techniques, the use of role plays requires good judgment and common sense. Role plays for new employees generally require the instructor to play the role of customer as new employees cannot realistically do this. Experienced employees playing the customer are often tempted to overdo the role, make the situation impossible, or take out their frustrations during the role play unless they are given some guidelines or a limited script.

Role plays are often boring for students not directly involved and thus are not suitable as a participative training technique for large groups of students or for use as the only training technique. Participation can be spread by asking students to prepare in workshop groups for the role play and by asking students not directly involved to make notes and report on specific assigned aspects of the role play. Trainers should see that students do not feel embarrassed but rather feel free to participate, including making mistakes. Role plays carried out in front of guest experts or visiting members of the management team create undue stress for students.

Role plays, of course, need to be realistic, to simulate real-life on-the-job situations, and to be used in the pursuit of agreed upon instructional objectives.

USING CASE STUDIES

Case studies are a way of taking students out of their immediate environment and forcing them to look in different ways at situations similar to their own. Case studies might be presented as in-basket exercises, as action mazes, or in workshop teams. They might be actual situations from the company with the names and locations changed to focus attention away from routine approaches. Or they might be actual situations from competitors or allied industries.

It is important for case studies to be realistic, and the best way to do this is to construct them with real data and situations. The anonymity of the situation allows students to try to place themselves in the situation and to think and feel it. Because it is not their own situation, they are encouraged to think creatively and speak their opinions openly. Case studies often prompt animated discussion when the solutions offered by the teams are shared.

Case studies are more effectively used for experienced employees than for new employees as they allow students to actively use their experience and knowledge. Case studies are particularly useful for combining front-line service delivery situations and back-office service support situations so that both groups of employees understand each other and gain a feeling for the important relationship and critical interaction between the two.

USING FILMS AND VIDEOTAPES

Audio-visual techniques such as films and videotapes produce variety in the classroom environment, and students generally enjoy them.

Commercially available films and videotapes may be rented or purchased to demonstrate service delivery situations that could not otherwise be shown in the classroom and to make points that might otherwise be made only in lecture. Effective use can be made by introducing the film or videotape to students and asking them to be accountable for noting specific items or elements for subsequent discussion.

Many companies make their own films and videotapes for use in the training process. While this can be expensive, particularly effective training tools can be the result. A company making a film or videotape should use professional techniques. Students are accustomed to viewing top-quality commercial videotapes and films and will not accept the home movie approach. A common idea is to record the company's employees "doing it wrong." A related idea is to make an amateur production of everything going wrong, generally enacted by nonprofessional actors. Good, bad, and average customer situations on the screen should be balanced so that students see all sides. Overdone wrong examples are insulting to employees. It is better to create thought-provoking realistic situations for discussion.

Films and videotapes made for a company's sales force, for television advertising, or for promotional purposes can also be useful to trainers.

FREQUENCY OF TRAINING

Technical skills and behavioral skills training should be given to new employees to help them do their new jobs with confidence and to produce customer satisfaction. Skills training is necessary as often as new technical skills are required to handle new product offerings, new computer systems, job rotations, promotions, advances in technology, and changes to technical procedures. Behavioral skills training is also necessary as often as new behavioral skills are required to handle new service offerings, new service delivery techniques as a result of automation or product changes, job rotations, promotions, competitive actions, and changes to service procedures.

Because good customer contact skills often depend on attitude, a good case can be made for regularly bringing customer contact employees into the classroom for discussion of improved service delivery and customer satisfaction. Results of employee attitude surveys can be used to determine the areas of greatest concern to employees. Results of customer satisfaction surveys and customer complaint letters can be used to pinpoint areas in need of improvement as can audit reports and quality assurance reports.

Training is generally defined as an organized activity that produces a change in behavior. Other related methods may be used, such as roadshows, quality circles, meetings, seminars, new product launches, and pep rallies, to spark attitude and behavior changes that improve service delivery. Most employees, when surveyed, will say that they receive value from these gatherings and that they would like more.

USING EXTERNAL CONSULTANTS

External consultants offer a variety of fresh new ideas and approaches to assist the training effort and may be used in several ways.

They may be a source of new ideas to the in-house training staff. Or they may train the in-house training staff to conduct a specified off-the-shelf program. External consultants can develop a company-specific training program (or modify an off-the-shelf program to suit the company's needs) and then train the in-house training staff to conduct it. They may also be used to conduct the training.

Outside consultants may have an advantage in recommending changes to senior management. Because management is keenly aware of how much money is being spent on the consultant's services, management may be more receptive to the recommendations.

Care must be taken to select consultants and external courses that agree with the company's service strategy. Time and money may have to be spent to bring the consultant to a sufficient level of understanding of the company's products and services, management style, and values. Clear and accurate briefing of a consultant, spelling out specific measurable objectives and results in a contract, help a company obtain maximum benefit.

Excellent service companies generally have a formal and organized training approach that covers all employees at various stages in their careers. An external consultant hired to carry out a specific training program needs to be integrated into the overall training approach. If a consultant conducts a customer contact training course for all employees, how will new employees receive this course in the future? If the consultant is creating modules of training for the in-house training staff to use in training new employees, is it important to give this training to existing employees with six months or six years of experience and, if so, how will this be done (and what will justify the cost)?

ON-THE-JOB TRAINING

Many of today's large corporations have found that training centers and formal classroom training provide the most cost-effective means of turning out large numbers of trained personnel.

On-the-job training is a broad term that can be applied to the personal guidance and instruction an employee receives at the work station after attending a formal training program at a company training center, to the ongoing guidance and development that occurs each day on the job, to an apprentice system, or to the one-on-one training given to an employee in an organization without a formal training program.

On-the-job training can be an effective training method. It has four steps:

1. The on-the-job trainer explains the steps or techniques and then demonstrates the steps or techniques.

2. The on-the-job student explains the steps or techniques while the on-the-job trainer demonstrates or follows the student's instructions.

3. The student explains the steps or techniques and demonstrates.

4. The student repeats the explanation and demonstration for the trainer until both are satisfied the activity has been learned.

On-the-job training is not, therefore, a silent activity. The student must be able to verbally repeat the procedure as well as perform it.

One of the greatest difficulties of on-the-job training is finding a time and a place for it. In the service delivery arena, it is particularly difficult if customers observe the training. Programmed learning, job aids, and computer-based instructional materials help ensure consistency in on-the-job training and make the trainer's job easier, but time and place for discussion are prime obstacles.

On-the-job training is not a substitute for management discipline or for auditing or quality assurance. Years ago at Avis in some countries, on-the-job trainers traveled from station to station explaining the correct procedures wherever they observed wrong practices, only to return six months later to find employees following the same wrong practices. Trainers cannot perform the daily management discipline function on behalf of the managers.

PERSONAL DEVELOPMENT

Swissair's in-flight magazine describes the quality of its apprenticeship programs for bakers, chefs, electronics technicians, mechanics, office clerks, and others, which supplement its formal training programs for air hostesses and pilots. "Great importance is attached not only to teaching job skills but also to the apprentice's personal development. Because satisfied bakers or mechanics make for satisfied customers. And in the case of Swissair, this means satisfied passengers."

Development is a lifelong process of personal growth in knowledge, skill, and attitude. Development is also the way in which a company can obtain unmeasured but dynamic synergy from its human resource assets.

To develop employees they must have opportunities: company training courses, encouragement of outside education, the chance to voluntarily participate in suitable projects and assignments, praise for good behavior, explanations of company decisions, rotation or promotion to desired jobs, help in identifying weaknesses and ways to develop skills.

Bernhard Vaschauner managed the Hotel Lanserhof from 1980 until 1983, taking over the running of this 150-bed hotel near Innsbruck, Austria, when he was only 26 years old. In addition to building conference business and turning the hotel from loss to profit, Vaschauner hired many young people and provided them with the opportunity to grow and develop in their jobs. He spent long hours with his young team educating them in the hotel and conference business. Repeat conference organizers returned again and again to the hotel because Vaschauner and his staff were willing to do everything possible, even at short notice, to make the conference a success. There were no rule or procedure books, only a commitment to providing whatever was wanted. Employees were urged to pitch in and help in any crisis, whether it was "their job" or not.

After the Hotel Lanserhof was turned into a health resort in 1983, many of Vaschauner's staff went on to successful businesses or careers. Eva Zelger, Vaschauner's assistant manager, founded a successful café in the university area with a partner. Otto Sardinia, Vaschauner's bartender, manages the dining room of the Altstadt-stueberl. Werner Pichler, a trainee waiter hired by Vaschauner when he was only 16, works at the Intercontinental Hotel in Berlin. Franz Kaufmann, Vaschauner's chef, opened a successful guest house and café and later a successful café with his wife Brigitte. Herbert and Christl Freitag, who managed and worked in Vaschauner's main dining room, managed a guest house in Klagenfurt and now have their own in Styria.

GUIDELINES FOR CHIEF EXECUTIVES

When British Airways implemented its "putting people first" training program for all staff, Sir Colin Marshall, chief executive, made a personal appearance at more than half of the sessions.

Winston V. Morrow, Jr., when he was president and chief executive officer of Avis, spent three days each year renting and checking in cars. Before each of his visible management periods, he went through the training program for Avis rental sales agents.

David Longridge, former general manager of Avis International, wanted to implement a performance appraisal system. The first staff to undergo training, at Longridge's insistence, were Longridge and his management team.

Many chief executives believe in training and development, actively oversee its progress and encourage participation, and insist on their own participation and involvement. One of the more significant support actions a chief executive can take is to ensure that supervisors and managers moving up through the ranks attend supervisory skills and management skills training programs before they supervise or manage the company's human resources. Another is to support the policy that new employees receive training before they serve customers. A third is to put one's foot down on last-minute cancellations and withdrawals from company training programs, often where "working on a project for the chief executive" is the prime excuse.

There is always the management concept of mirror image: what the chief executive says and does is mirrored down the line. If chief executives provide training and development opportunities to direct subordinates, and take the time to explain decisions to direct subordinates so that they grow and develop, then there is a greater chance that these attitudes are mirrored down the line.

GUIDELINES FOR FRONT-LINE SERVICE DELIVERY PERSONNEL

Front-line service delivery personnel are often at the mercy of the company's management with regard to the available training and development opportunities. But these employees can ask themselves the following:

1. Do I readily volunteer for or ask to attend all company training programs for which I'm eligible?

2. When I attend company training programs, do I participate fully and use the opportunity to gain maximum skills and knowledge?

3. When I do not understand a decision or new procedure, do I ask my manager or colleagues for clarification?

4. When I understand a decision or new procedure, do I help my colleagues to understand it?

5. Do I consider my own personal development important and undertake activities and courses on my own time to contribute to my service career?

GUIDELINES FOR BACK-OFFICE SERVICE SUPPORT PERSONNEL

Back-office service support personnel often feel that management offers them few training and development opportunities. They may even feel that the few opportunities that do exist favor front-line service delivery personnel. However, they can ask themselves the following questions:

1. Do I readily volunteer for or ask to attend all company training programs for which I'm eligible?

2. When I attend company training programs, do I participate fully and use the opportunity to gain maximum skills and knowledge?

3. When I do not understand a decision or new procedure, do I ask my manager or colleagues for clarification?

4. When I understand a decision or new procedure, do I help my colleagues to understand it?

5. Do I consider my own personal development important and undertake activities and courses on my own time to contribute to my career?

GUIDELINES FOR MIDDLE MANAGEMENT

Middle managers can mirror downwards the management style and priorities of senior management. They have significant power to support the training effort and to create development opportunities for employees. It is often middle managers who enroll staff in training courses and rearrange schedules and priorities to allow staff to attend courses. It is often middle managers who cancel staff enrollments in training courses and who withdraw staff in the middle of courses to handle urgent priorities. It is often middle managers across a wide variety of functional areas who provide the input for needs analysis and course content to the training department. And it is often middle managers who go off in their own direction to hire an external consultant to carry out an isolated training activity inconsistent with the company's training approach and service strategy.

Middle management carries a significant burden of responsibility and accountability in training and developing people to deliver service, and middle managers should ask themselves:

1. Do I enroll my employees and myself in all company training courses for which we are eligible and that are appropriate?

2. Do I rearrange schedules and priorities so that my employees and I can participate fully in courses we attend?

3. Do I discuss the course objectives and their importance with my employees before they attend a course so that they are prepared positively to take maximum advantage of the course?

4. Do I review what has been learned and how it will apply on the job with employees when they return from a training course?

5. Do I send new employees to training courses or give them adequate on-the-job training before asking them to perform their new job or serve customers?

6. Am I familiar with what is taught to my employees in company training courses and do I support and reinforce the training given? If there is a procedure or technique being taught that I don't agree with, do I try to resolve this disagreement with the training department?

7. Do I actively contribute to the design and content of training programs for my employees?

8. Do I encourage my employees to develop themselves?

9. When my employees face a new procedure, service, product, or decision, do I try to explain and help them fully understand it?

10. Do I have and follow an action plan for my own development?

6

Deliver Perception of a Superior Product

In the center of the picturesque resort village of Seefeld in Austria stands a handpainted building in the Tirolean style. It houses the Tiroler Schmuckkastl, a jewelry store owned and run by Guenther and Rosi Armbruster.

Handpainted Tirolean decorations surround the six display windows that show off a wide variety of jewelry, watches, ivory, and figurines in all price ranges. One can purchase a $10,000 diamond ring, bring in a precious stone for an exquisite design and setting, buy a $24 ivory ring, bring in a priceless piece of antique jewelry or a $20 bracelet to be cleaned, purchase a $5 brooch, or one can simply take in the display windows, stroll through the elegant small shop, and pick up a postcard to send home. Each piece of jewelry and merchandise will be treated and handled with care, as if it were the most expensive piece in the shop. In the quaint and charming display windows, one feels an impression of quality, good craftsmanship, and elegance in even the least expensive item.

The decor and design of the shop, the ambiance and atmosphere inside, the merchandise itself, and the service delivery techniques, actions, and words of the Armbrusters bespeak quality, elegance, and individual warmth. They create the customer's perception that a piece of jewelry purchased, cleaned, or designed in this shop is very special, like no other. The Tiroler Schmuckkastl delivers the perception of a superior product to first-time tourists as well as to their many repeat customers.

IMAGE AND IMPRESSION

A Rolex watch, a Rolls Royce motor car, dinner at Tour D'Argent in Paris, a flight on Concorde, a Louis Vuitton suitcase, Chanel No. 5 perfume, a set of Rosenthal china, a weekend at the Plaza in New York: all evoke an image and impression of quality and elegance, the best there is.

Advertising and promotional money goes into developing the desired image and impression of a product or service in the minds of consumers. Money also goes into developing a product or service and ensuring that it is produced to desired quality standards. It is difficult in today's marketplace to survive without investment in both elements. It is difficult to simply become known as offering the best-quality product or service without advertising and promotion, or to create a lasting image and impression of quality when products or services are indeed faulty.

Image and impression are elusive qualities. Image and impression of superior quality are often generated by television or print advertising, a classic example being that of popular perfumes and fragrances. Image and impression of superior quality are shaped by other methods as well, such as price, since consumers expect to pay a premium price for a premium product or service; the surroundings in which the product or service is delivered to customers; and the attitude and manner of service delivery personnel as they deliver the product or service to customers.

People who order a Mercedes for pick up at the main production plant in Sindelfingen, Germany, find themselves at "what is probably the world's only combination hotel and service center for new car owners, complete with sleeping facilities, a bar, two restaurants, two 100-seat film theaters, four conference rooms, even a diaper-changing area for families bringing their babies along for their first ride" (*Time,* June 22, 1987).

This issue of *Time,* in an article subtitle, "Steep prices are no problem for West Germany's quality exports," described West Germany's record export surplus.

West Germans have achieved this export miracle by charging top prices for expensively produced goods made within their own borders. West German manufacturers believe it is the product itself, not the promotional sizzle, that sells their wares. Meinhard Miegel, director of the Institute for Economic and Social Policy in Bonn says: "By not assembling our products from plants all over the world, we can ensure that they have quality and integrity that comes from having the same people building them for years. We like our products to feel as if they come from one pair of hands. A lot of people are willing to pay a premium for that."

WORD-OF-MOUTH ADVERTISING

Image and impression are also created by word-of-mouth advertising, which is simply consumers telling other consumers of their experiences and impressions—both good and bad. It is a powerful method of advertising but not one in which the company can control the message. According to studies done by TARP, dissatisfied customers tell twice as many people about their experience as do satisfied customers.

In some markets, word-of-mouth advertising carries great power. An example is the word-of-mouth experiences passed between frequent business travelers regarding specific flights, hotels in specific cities, and car rentals in specific cities. At Avis in Europe, a market research study showed that one of the more significant factors influencing which car rental company to use on vacation was friends' recommendations.

The only defenses appear to be that a company aims for 100 percent satisfied customers and has a strong advertising message that is easily repeated by satisfied customers to their friends.

TESTING CUSTOMER PERCEPTION

An array of methods have successfully been used to test customer perception. One is market research. Another is the widespread use of toll-free telephone numbers to solicit complaints and ideas for product or service improvement. Customer comment cards, customer satisfaction surveys, and customer satisfaction tracking systems also provide hard data. John Goodman and Arlene Malech of TARP describe a vivid example.

> Complaint data on a Polaroid camera in the mid-1970s showed that customers were not replacing worn-out camera batteries. The result was customer frustration and dissatisfaction because the camera didn't work. This information was relayed to product development and the camera was modified so that the battery was contained in the film pack. Thus, each time a new film pack was inserted, the battery was automatically changed. The result was happier customers and increased film sales.

Customer complaint letters and calls plus complaints or inquiries voiced at the point of sale also provide data on customer perception. The most important point is to use some method to test customer perception of the product or service being delivered and to use that information to modify and adapt the product or service to fit customers' needs or perceived needs.

TESTING EMPLOYEE PERCEPTION

Employee perception of the product or service being delivered should be tested because employee views have a way of expressing themselves clearly during the service delivery process.

Employee surveys, focus groups, quality circles, and suggestion programs can solicit employee views. In some situations, employees may be asked to use the product or service as customers and evaluate it.

Most important is to use *some* method to test employee perception of the product or service being delivered and to use that information to modify and adapt the product or service to better fit employees' perceptions of customer needs.

SERVICE STRATEGY

A company's service strategy has an impact on customer and employee perception, particularly where a service rather than a product is being featured. Customers go to McDonald's for fast, friendly service in a clean environment at a reasonable price; if they were hungry for the world's best hamburger, they'd probably make it themselves over the backyard barbeque grill. Because service strategy helps create perception of a superior product or service it is often featured in advertising and publicity materials.

CHANGING PERCEPTION

The most obvious way to change perception so that customers and potential customers have the image and impression that a company is delivering a superior product or service is for the company to deliver a superior product or service 100 percent of the time and widely advertise the fact. This is not often a realistic course of action for most companies, although most consumers do expect this performance from airlines, health and medical services, and nuclear power plants.

Improvements in service and changes in customers' and employees' perceptions are generally the result of many actions and hard work on many fronts over a long period of time. In fact, the process never stops unless the marketplace stops needing the product or service.

One of TARP's most significant findings is that customers are more likely to purchase a product or service again if they have been asked their opinion or given an easy way to express a complaint, even if their opinion is never acknowledged or their complaint is not answered or not answered satisfactorily. This means that companies can immediately take a step toward improving customer perception by asking customers for their opinions and comments and by encouraging complaints and questions from customers. Following this, of course, companies will want to take further steps to correct problems experienced and to answer complaints and questions in such a way that a higher and higher percentage of customers will want to purchase the product or service again.

Market research is essential to measure changes in perception and to get at what customers really want. In the past, much attention in market research was focused on the product, leading companies to develop new products and make improvements in existing products. Companies with a commitment to superior service are beginning to use these same vital market research techniques to focus on service. As Mike Bruce, senior development projects manager for British Airways, writes in his *ICT* (March/April 1987) article entitled "Managing People First—Bringing the Service Concept to British Airways":

> When British Airways' chief executive, Colin Marshall, decided to do something about customer service, there was no substantial up-to-date psychographic data on what fundamentally moved our customers. This was partly a consequence of operating in a noncompetitive environment. There was also the bureaucratic culture that had developed under government ownership. In part it was a consequence of priority given to operational efficiency at the expense of marketing effectiveness but more deeply I suspect it was a failure to see the airline as a "service" industry, understand the implications of that and act upon it.

The news media in the United States have a powerful impact on customer and employee perception of product and service quality.

On the negative side, some companies and industries live in fear of having their practices and policies exposed in a less than favorable light to millions of customers who view "60 Minutes" or of having a consumer advocate like Ralph Nader begin to investigate their industry. On the positive side, companies like Merck gain a positive effect on perception from press releases on the success of new drugs. While new drugs are developed to make money for a company, they are perceived as having a humanitarian purpose. Perception is also influenced more subtly through other public relations activities, such as having one's product or service used by leading characters in a successful movie or obtaining press coverage for sponsorship of humanitarian and community service projects and programs.

Awards and recognition received by a company also contribute to customer and employee perceptions and changes in these perceptions. The Avis training department won the National Training Award in the United Kingdom in 1987, receiving press coverage and building the perception of a company committed to training its service employees. Direct service awards, such as being voted best of the year, also change perception.

GUIDELINES FOR CHIEF EXECUTIVES

In some companies, chief executives personally contribute to the perception of superior product or service. Frank Borman, perceived as one of America's heroic astronauts, appeared in television commercials as chief executive of Eastern Airlines, creating the subtle impression that America's skills in flying through outer space had been put to work running ordinary airplanes. Frank Perdue effectively sold his company's chickens in early television commercials by creating the perception that he was a simple, good chicken farmer.

Chief executives play a key role in delivering the perception of a superior product or service. Chief executives need to consider the following:

1. Does my company's advertising create the perception of superior product or service?

2. Do my company's promotional and public relations activities lead to the perception of a superior product or service?

3. Do I regularly know how my company's customers perceive my company's products and services?

4. Do I regularly know how my company's employees perceive my company's products and services?

5. Do the surroundings in which my company's products and services are delivered contribute to an image and impression of a superior product and service in the minds of customers and employees?

6. Do I engage myself and other employees of my company in external activities (conferences, seminars, press conferences, awards, etc.) that add to my company's overall image of superior products and services?

GUIDELINES FOR FRONT-LINE SERVICE DELIVERY PERSONNEL

Front-line service delivery personnel play a vital role in creating the impression of a superior product or service. The way the Armbrusters at the Tiroler Schmuckkastl handle and show a piece of jewelry, whether it costs $10 or $10,000, tells the customer that the product is superior. The enthusiasm with which the bartenders at the Hotel Klosterbraeu in Seefeld, Austria, roll into action to deliver a proper breakfast to a guest who has missed breakfast bespeaks their belief that they are delivering the guest a superior service.

Front-line service delivery personnel need to ask themselves:

1. Do I believe in the products and services I am delivering to customers and do I act accordingly with customers?

2. Do I actively contribute ideas for product and service improvement through the channels open to me?

3. Am I able to defend the quality of my company's products and services to customers and friends?

4. Do I represent my company and its products and services well whenever I'm called upon to do so?

GUIDELINES FOR BACK-OFFICE SERVICE SUPPORT PERSONNEL

Back-office service support personnel play a significant role in helping to create the impression of a superior product or service, for it is often the work done by service support personnel that contributes directly to product quality or enables good service to be given. The skill and consistency with which McDonald's hamburgers are made by service support personnel or the cleanliness of the glasses washed by service support personnel in a restaurant contribute to the customers' perception of a superior product and service.

Back-office service support personnel need to ask themselves:

1. Do I believe in the products and services my company is delivering to customers?

2. Do I understand the importance of my job to the perception of a superior product or service?

3. Do I actively contribute ideas for product and service improvement through the channels open to me?

4. Am I able to defend the quality of my company's products and services to customers and friends?

5. Do I represent my company and its products and services well whenever I'm called upon to do so?

GUIDELINES FOR MIDDLE MANAGEMENT

Middle managers are substantially responsible for creating the impression of a superior product or service. Recommendations for product or service enhancement often end up on a middle manager's desk to die or move forward to action. Reports of customer perceptions and employee perceptions of service and product delivery often reach the desks of middle managers.

In the vast range of jobs in middle management fall the positions that approve or disapprove advertising briefs, the positions that give priority to public relations and community relations activities, the positions that speak to the press, the positions that approve or disapprove capital expenditures to refurbish offices and service delivery points and to outfit company employees in uniforms. Middle managers often speak externally on behalf of the company, lead departments that win awards, and represent the company at public events.

Middle managers in all functional areas should consider:

1. Do I believe in my company and its products and services?

2. Do I do everything within my power to help my company deliver the perception of a superior product or service?

3. Do I represent the company and its products and services well in every contact with customers, employees, and the general public?

7

Gear Performance to Deliver Service as a Number One Priority

Jane remembered Mother's Day just two days before. She called the exclusive women's shop, Yvonne's of Camp Hill, Pennsylvania, from Chicago and asked them to send her mother, who lived about fifteen miles from the shop, a pair of slacks and a blouse. The next day, Kathleen Lineberger, a sales clerk at Yvonne's of Camp Hill, drove to Jane's mother's home and delivered a beautifully wrapped package to Jane's mother.

Madelyn needed a cocktail dress for a party and had no time to shop until the day of the party. She went to Yvonne's of Camp Hill where Rose, who did alterations, rearranged priorities and worked late so that Madelyn had a perfectly fitting dress in time.

John left his Christmas shopping for female relatives until the last minute, arriving just two hours before closing time on Christmas

Eve at Yvonne's of Camp Hill. Yvonne Nelson, the owner, kept the shop open and employees on duty wrapping packages until a very satisfied John left with all the gifts he needed, beautifully wrapped.

These are routine services at Yvonne's of Camp Hill, where service is a number one priority for all employees.

PERFORMANCE STANDARDS

In the manufacturing era, product standards evolved to guarantee and check the quality of each product coming off the assembly line. As we evolve into a service era, guaranteeing and checking the quality of each service delivery have provided an even greater challenge.

Many service companies talk in terms of performance standards, meaning the minimum acceptable level of service to be delivered. Answering the telephone within three rings is an example of a performance standard that brings an element of service from the intangible to the tangible and provides a measurable standard against which performance can be assessed, audited, and rewarded or corrected.

Some companies have taken performance standards further, following Robert Mager's approach (1962) to instructional objectives. Answering the telephone within three rings 90 percent of the time, or answering the telephone within three rings under normal conditions and within five rings in busy periods, are examples. Some companies have tried to legislate all service performance into standards. For example, during each customer contact, the employee will smile at least once, establish eye contact at least twice, and say, "Have a nice day." Again, these are measurable; performance can be assessed, audited, and rewarded or corrected.

Centralized reservation offices often operate with a call service factor or call service level of 85 percent, meaning that the computerized equipment measuring incoming calls registers the fact that 85 percent of calls are answered within 20 seconds. If the call service level drops below 85 percent, more agents are needed. If it goes above 85 percent, fewer agents are needed. In the early days of centralized reservation offices, managers and supervisors used to actively involve the agents in the call service level, using bells or lights to signal the number of calls waiting so that agents would know when to promptly move from one call to the next. Each shift or day, supervisors would let agents know the number of calls that had been handled and the call service level achieved.

Unfortunately, the call service level became translated into a performance standard when, in fact, it is a budgetary standard for pinpointing staffing levels in a centralized reservation office. To customers, knowing that 85 percent of their calls will be answered within 20 seconds is hardly a service standard viewed as superior or excellent. Its logic eludes agents themselves who are not completely familiar with the return on investment or cost of a 95 percent or 100 percent call service level.

In *In Search of Excellence* (1982), Archie McGill of AT&T is quoted as saying, "Suppose you have a ninety-five percent standard. What about the five percent? Even though one hundred percent may be theoretically unattainable, the business ought to act as if any failure is intolerable." Each individual perceives service in his or her own terms, and any business engaged in delivering service needs to understand this.

Performance standards must be based on what customers expect. Just as customers want a product without defects, so do they want service without defects. Even if zero defects is what the customer expects and a company finds this too expensive to achieve, the goal or performance standard should be zero defects if that is what customers expect. What customers expect varies across industries, zero defects being the expectation of a patient about to undergo open-heart surgery, very different from the expectation of customers who stand in line for 45 minutes at a Disneyland ride.

Service companies have gone through performance standard phases. One phase was comparison with competitors. In England, calling an airline reservation office meant listening to at least 25 rings, whether it was a British, European, or American carrier. All of the competitors were offering similarly poor service. One competitor might try to outdo another by answering the phone within 23 rings, but would a customer notice the difference? While the service offered by competitors is still a keen concern to management, it is no longer a sign of excellent service to offer equally poor or slightly less poor service than the competitors.

Another period was the measurable standards phase with realistic or attainable targets. Answering the phone within three rings 90 percent of the time is an example, taking into account those extremely busy times when chaos rules the office and everybody has decided to call at once. These kinds of realistic or attainable targets with measurement variables are hardly inspirational to employees. They require standard performance rather than inspire exceptional performance.

On the other hand, saying the service standard is to answer the phone within three rings all of the time and then measuring success can produce exceptional performance. For example, if a group of employees performed at 93 percent last month and 94 percent this month, there is a sense of achievement far greater than knowing they achieved the 90 percent standard for both months. Performance is highest when there is a risk that the target cannot be achieved, and motivation is highest when the objective has only a 50 percent chance of success.

This leads us to the exceptional performance phase, a phase where performance standards inspire exceptional performance rather than dictating minimum performance and where customer expectations have the highest priority. The standard for telephone answering really becomes—answer the phone when the customers want us to, which is generally right away all of the time (with market research confirming what customers truly expect).

Performance standards should address two distinct situations: normal operating conditions, and extraordinary operating conditions when something has gone wrong.

Performance standards also should be flexible enough to allow employee creativity, the most flexible standard being the Hotel Klosterbraeu's rule to do whatever is necessary to make the guest happy. Many companies, however, require more detailed performance standards based on their marketplace, such as how long a customer waits for a Big Mac or how thick the sauce should be on a Domino's pizza, to support the consistency promised in their service strategies.

SETTING TARGETS AND AGREEING ON OBJECTIVES

Asking a manager how he or she knows when he or she is doing a good job, the likely answers are in terms of profit, revenue, profit improvement, revenue improvement, improved return on assets, increased return on investment, or any number of financial measurements. Managers may even respond in terms of industry-specific financial measurements, such as occupancy rate in the Sheraton Frankfurt Airport Hotel, table turnover in the Hilton's grill room, call service factor at American Airlines' reservation center, or market share at a Hertz airport rental station.

In exceptional service companies, answers are likely to deal more specifically with service: new products sold to existing accounts at IBM in Croydon, England, additional reservations placed by the Avis station in Stavanger, Norway, the number of complimentary letters received by Singapore Airlines. Some managers may even say that their level of customer satisfaction has improved by 2 percent, a statistic known from a customer satisfaction tracking system.

In superior service companies, targets and objectives are not purely financial but also include specific measures of service delivery, expressed in numeric or financial terms where possible. Customer satisfaction and service delivery matter in these companies, and many make these targets and objectives top priority.

In the past, commonly accepted measures were traditional factors such as revenue and profit. Few companies have had ways of measuring service delivery and customer satisfaction. Some companies used the only method that has historically been available: the number of complaints and compliments received by a customer service department. At Avis in the United States, a simple quality report was used to rank districts based on the scores they received on the most recent quality assurance visit, number of complaints received, most recent market share, and scored results from customer comment cards. Position changes on the report were added to targets and objectives for performance appraisal, incentive plans, and recognition programs.

Targets and objectives should include service delivery and customer satisfaction, and these should be at the top rather than at the bottom of the list. Not to do so delivers a clear message to employees regarding the priority of service delivery and customer satisfaction. Targets and objectives should also be agreed on with the full participation and involvement of employees.

JOB DESCRIPTIONS

Job descriptions should reflect the service role and the elements of customer satisfaction. Without them, superior service delivery appears to employees as "nice to have" rather than "need to have."

Some companies even focus entirely on these activities, relegating those activities not in support of customer satisfaction to lesser priority or leaving them out of the job description completely. Says Glenn Van Heerden, managing director of Avis in South Africa, "If you take care of your customers, the revenue and profit will take care of themselves."

Job descriptions need clearly defined duties so that employees understand expectations. But they need to allow flexibility and creativity on the part of the employees. Job descriptions are often written to obtain higher grade levels, salaries, and benefits for the jobs or to satisfy the personnel department. The personnel department needs to be brought into the service strategy of the company so that they understand the critical importance of the jobs that serve customers and the jobs that support service delivery.

In particular, service delivery jobs need to include the element of serving customers, and the scope needs to be sufficiently broad and the structure sufficiently flexible to allow superior service to happen. It is often the small extra touches that remain in customers' minds—the photograph taken for tourists by a waitress or porter, the enjoyable restaurant recommended by the gift shop clerk, a few kind words by a hospital cleaner to an elderly patient.

The job descriptions for back-office service support personnel should also reflect the customer element: how the job relates to the service being delivered, key duties of the job that contribute to customer satisfaction, why the job is needed in terms of customer satisfaction.

PRIORITIES

A loyal customer of Lufthansa Airlines wrote to its customer service department in London about the good service she received, but asked why her baggage kept coming off their airplanes with the baggage tags missing. In reply, she received a warm letter with an explanation of the automated baggage handling equipment which sometimes ripped off baggage tags. Enclosed with the letter were 24 Lufthansa baggage tags and a new leather wallet. Several years later, the same customer's baggage was broken into while checked with Lufthansa and $5,000 worth of jewelry stolen. When she reported the theft to Lufthansa, the company acknowledged with a terse letter of apology, claiming no responsibility for the theft. Another letter to the customer service department in London produced the same response. The customer, of course, stopped flying Lufthansa.

Airlines operate within strict national and international regulations, and their liability for theft generally does not include jewelry. However, excellent service companies bear the responsibility and accountability for delivering service as a top priority all, not just some, of the time. Satisfying customers must have top priority.

Setting priorities to serve and satisfy customers first sounds obvious and simple, but day-to-day it is a hard principle to follow. Below are some examples of other priorities taking precedence:

- An agent or clerk is closing out his or her cash drawer when a customer appears. The customer has to wait a few minutes while a new agent or clerk takes over or while this one finds a suitable place in the administrative process to stop.

- A service person finishes his or her conversation with a colleague before turning to serve a waiting customer.

- A supervisor releases several service delivery personnel for coffee breaks when customers are waiting.

- A company staffs and organizes a service delivery point so that an insufficient number of employees at peak times must simultaneously handle customers in person and on the telephone.

- A steady customer returns often, but service personnel do not recognize or acknowledge the repeat business.

- A receivables clerk delays posting a customer's mailed-in payment in order to help with the month-end closing, and the customer receives a dunning notice.

- A company changes its prices but fails to immediately update the price reference materials used by centralized sales offices. The legal department recommends stamping all customer materials with the notice "prices subject to change without notice."

- A marketing department develops and advertises a new product, but service delivery personnel are not advised.

- A systems department installs new software in the billing system without notifying the training department. Billing employees follow old procedures, and many customer bills are wrong during the first week.

These examples demonstrate situations where providing service to customers has temporarily lost place as the number one priority. It takes constant commitment, constant stating of that commitment, and constant demonstration of that commitment to keep customers satisfied and all of the organization's employees delivering service as a top priority. Dawn Bethe Frankfort, writing in U.S. Air's magazine (October 1986) about "Milkman with the Midas Touch"

Stew Leonard, says that "if the customers like something, Leonard wants to give it to them. In fact, etched in stone at the store's entrance are two dairy commandments: Rule 1—The customer is always right; Rule 2—If the customer is ever wrong, re-read Rule 1. Leonard sees to it that these rules are followed from the moment a customer arrives."

At Avis in South Africa, service delivery employees are instructed to serve customers as the top priority. Employees are trained and coached on mistakes. But an incident showing indifference to customers produces an immediate warning letter, and repeated indifference to customers results in termination.

In large companies with centralized headquarters, back-office service support personnel may never have contact with customers. But policy decisions are made and jobs are carried out in service support, often without mention of the customer or thought about impact on customers. Priorities here too must have the customer in mind.

PERFORMANCE APPRAISALS

One of the most powerful ways to reinforce a message of service commitment is to use measures of customer satisfaction in the performance appraisal process. Employees should be told from the beginning, in their job description, training, and everyday supervision, that serving customers is the number one priority, and the informal and formal performance appraisal process should reinforce this emphasis.

Performance appraisal is easiest where specific measurements are in place. Employees know routinely where they stand, and the formal performance appraisal is no surprise. Performance appraisal is hardest where there are no measures of customer satisfaction, where a supervisor or manager must make direct observation in order to judge the employee's performance.

Good performance appraisals rely upon good setting of targets and agreement on objectives as well as on challenging performance standards. Supervisors and managers in the service delivery function bear a responsibility to continually assemble concrete data on performance: making notes of comments by customers about service delivery employees, filing copies of complaint and complimentary letters about employees, making notes of direct observations. A more concrete measurement in some companies is a customer satisfaction tracking system in which customers evaluate service and where performance can be tracked back to individual employees or teams of employees.

Performance appraisals in the service industry, as in other industries, should be open discussions that reach agreement on performance. The discussions should focus on performance that individual employees can control. Company policies and procedures that get in the way of superior service delivery cannot be allowed to be the source of poor performance and must be eliminated. Outstanding achievements in service delivery should be discussed and reinforced during performance appraisals.

The performance appraisal process should include discussion of career progression and training and development needs. Because so many young people work in service delivery, often in their first job and for low wages, the performance appraisal process should be a vital time for giving guidance and direction and for helping these employees establish a career plan. Used as a guidance tool, the performance appraisal can help a company keep its brightest young people for full careers.

PROMOTIONS

The following exercise is from a training program on customer service.

Gruesti House of Fondue is a rapidly expanding chain of Swiss fondue restaurants started by Hans Gruesti of Kloten, Switzerland. Gruesti came to the United States on vacation about 15 years ago and was struck by the American fascination with fast food restaurants. He had the idea to offer Americans an alternative in the form of a fondue restaurant where friends and family could spend an entire evening talking and enjoying themselves over, for example, a cheese appetizer fondue with sourdough bread and small hot dogs, a steak and sauces main course fondue, and a fruit and chocolate sauce dessert fondue.

Gruesti went back to Switzerland and saved his money until he was able, about seven years ago, to come back to the United States and begin opening his restaurants. The first restaurant was immediately popular, and Gruesti was pleased with his success in getting Americans to slow down over dinner. He opened many more Gruesti Houses of Fondue, but about two years ago, business growth slowed to a halt as Gruesti failed to position his restaurants correctly in the marketplace for medium-priced family restaurants. Gruesti tried many of his competitors' restaurants and finally hit upon the idea of marketing his restaurants as an evening of entertainment for the whole family where everybody could sample friendly Swiss service. Swiss-style yodelers were provided for entertainment, the decor in the restaurants was made more elaborately Swiss, and the larger restaurants hired young people to dress up in costumes, posing as yodelers, goats, and cows to entertain the children. All employees were given customer contact training, and Gruesti himself drafted customer contact standards for employees in Gruesti Houses of Fondue. The idea was a success.

Despite rapid growth, Gruesti himself became involved in promotions and transfers in all of his restaurants, although he relied upon the recommendations of his area managers. The Gruesti House of Fondue in Harrisburg, Pennsylvania, needed a manager, and Gruesti had two recommendations from area managers for persons to fill the job. One area manager was recommending Marion Howe, currently assistant manager in the Pittsburgh restaurant. Another area manager was recommending Marc Feldmeth, currently assistant manager in the Philadelphia restaurant.

Marion Howe began working in the Pittsburgh restaurant, one of Gruesti's first restaurants, about three years ago as a costume person. Her performances as a friendly Swiss cow gained her a reputation throughout the Gruesti chain and brought many families back again and again to the Pittsburgh restaurant. Marion held down a full-time job as a receptionist in those days, posing as a Swiss cow only in the evenings, in order to care for her two children. After almost a year of performing as the Swiss cow, Marion asked if she could learn the other jobs in the restaurant, and was given this opportunity. She worked in the kitchen, helped with the accounting and billing, and worked as a waitress. When the assistant manager's job was offered to her, Marion accepted it and quit her job as a receptionist to work full-time on her career at Gruesti. Marion is being recommended by her area manager because of her popularity with both customers and staff and her own desire to get on in the organization.

Marc Feldmeth joined Gruesti's Philadelphia restaurant, one of the newest in the chain, almost a year ago as a management trainee. He has a university degree in business management and, as a management trainee, worked all of the jobs in the Philadelphia restaurant before being given the assistant manager's job about six months ago. Marc is an aggressive young manager who has implemented some innovative cost-saving ideas in the Philadelphia restaurant and organized the various jobs more efficiently so that the Philadelphia restaurant operates with about two less staff than other restaurants with the same volume and size. Marc is being recommended by his area manager because of his impressive record in the Philadelphia restaurant and his own desire to get on in the organization.

Based on this limited information about the two candidates, formulate your own opinion on which one is most suited for the Harrisburg job and why you think so. The Harrisburg restaurant is also new but is smaller in size and volume than the Philadelphia and Pittsburgh restaurants.

While in real life more facts and data would be obtained and evaluated, the exercise does pose a realistic dilemma about promotions. In many companies, promotions have gone in the past to the individuals who demonstrated outstanding technical skills performance in their jobs. But the behavioral skills to supervise or manage other people and the behavioral skills and attitudes to deliver superior service to customers or to perform a job with a focus on the customer as the first priority are strong considerations for promotion in companies committed to improving service delivery. Considering these points for promotions supports a service strategy and provides one more way of communicating a commitment to superior service throughout the organization.

DAILY SUPERVISION

Good daily supervision of the service delivery and service support functions is also essential in delivering superior service. Supervising the manufacturing process allows the supervisor to look at the product coming off the assembly line. But, as Robert E. Kelley says in *Manager's Journal,* October 1987 *(Wall Street Journal)* about services, "Most are intangible: You cannot see a lawyer's advice nor take home a waiter's behavior. Services are generally consumed when provided: Unlike a defective car that can be recalled, you cannot recall a blundered heart operation or a demeaning comment to a customer."

This means that supervisors must indeed supervise the service delivery and service support functions, and this supervision cannot be done in a private office or a headquarters office. It has to be done where the service assembly line is churning out its service: where employees are speaking to customers, where bills are being sent to customers, where customer complaints are being handled. Many service-oriented companies post signs at service delivery points telling the name of the manager on duty. Too often, the manager on duty can be found behind a closed door, buried in paperwork, and unable to see the service being delivered.

Harold worked a full day in London before catching the evening flight to New York. The flight was full and noisy and arrived late. Baggage delivery was slow, and going through customs seemed to take forever. Harold waited over 15 minutes for the bus from the car rental company where he had a confirmed reservation. The bus driver stared idly into space as Harold and two other customers struggled to get their baggage onto the bus. At the car rental service area, Harold joined the end of the line of about 15 customers. Two agents behind the counter seemed to be moving in slow motion, and the line didn't move at all. Customers in the front of the line began grumbling to each other that they had been there for an hour and a half. Finally, one confronted an agent.

"Where's the manager?" demanded the customer loudly and angrily.

"I don't know where the manager is," retorted one of the agents.

A sign displayed the name of the station manager on duty, but this person did not appear.

After Harold had been there for an hour and a half, a breathless young supervisor in car rental uniform came through the office to deliver keys and say that no cars would be ready for about two more hours.

Harold finally got a car—not the one he had ordered—after a total waiting time of two hours, in line. His subsequent investigation revealed that the station manager *was* on duty, in a back office with the door closed.

Constant supervision includes direct observation of customer satisfaction, direct intervention to explain and resolve problems, and visibility and accessibility to staff and customers. Praise can be given on the spot to shape employee behavior. Undesirable behavior can be reprimanded or reshaped, just before employees face a similar situation. Supervisors must strike a balance between supporting employees and satisfying customers when a problem occurs with customers present.

Dale rearranged his return flight from Lisbon and received an updated ticket from the airline ticket office. Arriving at the check-in counter, he was told to go to the ticket counter because the agent couldn't find his reservation in her computer. Dale located the ticket office on another floor, where an agent promptly and easily retrieved his reservation from the computer and made a print of it. The agent asked Dale if he could wait just one moment. The agent hailed a passing supervisor and a brief animated discussion in Portuguese ensued, giving Dale the rather distinct impression that the ticket agent was pointing out to a supervisor that the check-in agent had not done her job properly. The ticket agent gave Dale the print of his reservation and asked him to return to the check-in counter where the same check-in agent processed Dale's transaction without comment. Dale proceeded to the business club lounge where he was asked why the check-in agent hadn't given him a pass to get in.

This incident shows several service failures but especially letting the customer become involved in a dispute. A customer should also not be made to feel as if he or she has done something wrong. Good supervision satisfies customers and supports employees at the same time.

In his article "Poorly Served Employees Serve Customers Just as Poorly" in *Manager's Journal*, October 1987 *(Wall Street Journal)*, Robert E. Kelley makes the point that service employees "treat customers similar to the way they, as employees, are treated by management." In many organizations, "management treats employees as unvalued and unintelligent. The employees in turn convey the identical message to the customer." Kelley offers a solution: "If managers want to improve service quality they must treat employees the same way they want employees to treat customers."

GUIDELINES FOR CHIEF EXECUTIVES

At the Hotel Klosterbraeu in Seefeld, Austria, owner Midi Seyrling greets guests in the dining room while her eyes survey every element of service being delivered by her staff. In the Braeukeller, while the Trio Edelweiss perform they greet guests by name. All of the hotel's staff from the cooks to the chambermaids offer a greeting to guests—in the hotel or on the streets when they're off duty.

Chief executives are responsible for observing service and customer satisfaction and for communicating the service strategy throughout the organization. Chief executives are also accountable for the management style that is mirrored downward all the way to the treatment of customers.

Chief executives should consider the following:

1. Does my company's service strategy clearly spell out the importance of satisfying customers and is the service strategy known at all levels in the organization?

2. Do performance standards in my company gear performance to deliver service as a number one priority and do they inspire exceptional performance?

3. Do I conduct performance appraisals with my direct line staff and do these performance appraisals focus on elements of customer satisfaction?

4. Do I manage and lead my staff in the way that, down the line, I would like to see my company's customers treated?

GUIDELINES FOR FRONT-LINE SERVICE DELIVERY PERSONNEL

At Pizza Hut in Bracknell, England, head waitress Pat refuses tips from her regular customers. At the Hotel Klosterbraeu in Seefeld, Austria, barman Juergen Spiss tells a customer, "We don't take tips from friends." At the En Vogue newsstand in Seefeld, Austria, owner Ewald Neururer and his employee Christina offer customers a Schnapps when the newspaper they've ordered has not been delivered.

Front-line service delivery employees hold the key to customer satisfaction, to the little extra touches that remain in customers' minds, to the efficient service that brings customers back. These employees also bear the burden of the organization's management style, performance standards, and conflicting priorities.

Kerstin, a car rental employee at a small station in Sweden, attended a training course on station selling skills. She asked the instructor from England whether it was correct policy for her to keep the station open late to serve a customer with a confirmed reservation when a flight was delayed. The car rental company did not pay her for this time, but that wasn't her concern. She simply wanted confirmation that she was doing the right thing. Employees should always know the service strategy and the performance expected of them.

Front-line service delivery personnel should consider the following:

1. Do I try to deliver service to customers as a number one priority? Do I do this even if my efforts appear to go unnoticed by my management?

2. Do I understand and know the performance standards for my job?

3. Do I have a job description or know what my job description is?

4. Do I fully participate in the performance appraisal process and obtain maximum benefit from it?

5. Do I make it as easy as possible for my supervisor or manager to help me with a customer problem?

6. Do I accept both praise and constructive criticism from my supervisor or manager?

GUIDELINES FOR BACK–OFFICE SERVICE SUPPORT PERSONNEL

At the Old Beams Kennels in Holyport, England, employees romp and jump with dogs during the dogs' exercise period. Employees pet cats and talk to them.

In the kitchen of a hotel, a dishwasher carefully checks each glass coming out of the dishwasher to see that the rims are not chipped or cracked. In the stock room of a catalogue sales company, packers carefully fulfill customer orders and pack them for safe shipment, double-checking that the correct item has been supplied. In a beauty salon, a junior assistant promptly and routinely sweeps cut hair from the floor.

Front-line service delivery employees often rely upon the jobs performed by back-office service support personnel. As a result, both groups hold the key to customer satisfaction, to the extras that remain in customers' minds, to the total service that brings customers back. Also, both groups bear the burden of the management style, performance standards, and conflicting priorities.

Back-office service support personnel should consider the following:

1. Do I try to perform each of my job duties to the best of my ability?

2. Do I understand and know the performance standards for my job?

3. Do I have a job description or know what my job description is?

4. Do I fully participate in the performance appraisal process and obtain maximum benefit from it?

5. When priorities conflict, do I choose those to do first which I know lead to greatest customer satisfaction? Do I do this even if my efforts appear to go unnoticed by my management?

GUIDELINES FOR MIDDLE MANAGEMENT

Middle management is responsible and accountable for making service delivery top priority by establishing challenging performance standards, by setting targets and agreed upon objectives that stimulate exceptional service performance, by defining jobs in terms of customer satisfaction balanced with company profits, by conducting good performance appraisals, by considering supervisory, leadership, and customer satisfaction skills when selecting candidates for promotion, by setting priorities and making decisions that consistently focus on customer satisfaction.

At the same time, middle management must follow the mandates and priorities set from above. The diversity of positions in middle management makes it difficult to produce a checklist of considerations for middle managers. The best overall consideration for middle managers is to ask, for each decision, for each course of action being taken, for the routine setting of priorities each day, if it gears performance to deliver service as the first priority.

8

Continuously Create the Opportunity for People to Deliver Superior Service

Just outside the Hotel Klosterbraeu in Seefeld, Austria, stands the "Siglu," a glass igloo-style bar, the idea of Sigi Seyrling and winner of the European Design Award for 1987. The Siglu vibrates with music, either from a lively array of tapes or from the varied talents of Jessy and Bocker. It usually looks impossible to squeeze more people in. When Jessy and Bocker entertain, using piano, bongo drums, maracas, guitar, or whatever else is handy, a customer has no choice but to clap hands and bounce with the music. Two friendly young women serve beer, wine, and cocktails from behind the circular bar. The Siglu is open from 3:00 P.M. until 1:00 A.M. each day in season. Jessy and Bocker provide live music twice during the 10-hour day for no more than one hour each time, but Jessy is on duty for all of those hours (plus set-up time), his job being to talk to customers and make sure they enjoy themselves. Faces are remembered at the Siglu. A guest need only return for the second time to be greeted by the two waitresses and receive a hearty welcome from Jessy, coupled with a bit of conversation, no matter how busy the Siglu is.

STAFFING

If asked, the front-line service delivery personnel in many companies would say that they don't have enough time to spend with customers, and that there aren't enough staff to deliver superior service. Few service employees would say they have an easy job with time to think about service.

The Siglu is staffed to comply with its service strategy of providing a cozy and friendly meeting place that really swings. Management considers necessary the level of staffing when preparing the business and profit plan. The strategy works and can be seen in action as each arrival squeezes through the door and is greeted by Jessy, Bocker, Monika, and Gudrun. Although the employees are busy and must work hard, the Siglu has sufficient staff to deliver service with friendly conversation.

Many people in the service industry, at all levels, blame poor service on the staffing levels dictated by budgets and profit goals. Staffing levels are important, as the Siglu's success shows, but there are other considerations.

At the Astir Palace Hotel in Vouliagmeni, Greece, a company held a business conference. On one night, a formal dinner for twenty-five of the top executives was scheduled for the most formal dining room in the hotel. As this company had held many such conferences in the hotel, the hotel's management knew this was an important dinner. Old tuxedos were pressed into service to outfit some of the porters and other hotel staff as waiters. While the food was acceptable, the service delivered by twenty waiters to twenty-five customers was poor by any standard. Untrained, unskilled staff provided slow, obtrusive, and sloppy service.

Many service companies have to deal with peaks such as the 11:00 A.M. and 2:00 P.M. rush of calls in a centralized reservation office, and seasonality, such as in tourist resorts. Often, untrained temporary or part-time help is employed to serve peak periods and seasons. This practice contributes to poor service of customers but also places stress on regular employees to answer questions, correct mistakes, and watch the service levels they strive so hard to maintain deteriorate.

During the budget process staffing levels should be considered not just in terms of profit but also in concert with the service strategy. Additional staffing should produce additional customer satisfaction and additional business from satisfied customers. Saving money by using part-time and temporary help may be offset by the cost of dissatisfied customers, the negative word-of-mouth advertising they spread, and the business they take elsewhere. It may also be negated by the impact it has on the productivity and service delivered by full-time permanent employees.

TEAM SPIRIT

Team spirit never appears as an asset on a company's balance sheet, yet it can contribute to superior service delivery by both back-office service support and front-line service delivery personnel.

Team spirit is observed and noticed by customers; so is its lack, particularly when service delivery employees appear to be working at odds with each other or when one area of an organization blames another for a malfunction.

Michael Leapman, writing in *Expression!* (1987) about British Airways and "How Colin Marshall makes it work," describes the attack made on service levels and team spirit with the "Putting People First" seminars and the "A Day in the Life" seminars. "The seminar stressed the importance of communication and inter-relationships between people—customers, managers and staff," Marshall explained. "One of the problems of large organizations, where you have many thousands of people all in one place, is that you become compartmentalized. They operate and meet only within their own functional lines. It's essential that they have more contact with others in the organization." Marshall says that at the end of seminars, "we adjourn to the bar and I mix with them and they can ask me questions directly. It's all part of the effort to get people to feel they're part of a total family."

Creating team spirit is easily carried out by some companies or specific units within a company. A good service strategy helps to create a central goal for team spirit. Training seminars and meetings as well as quality circles can be used to build team spirit. Although employees must be treated as individuals—with a balance between the task, the team, and the individual as put forth by John Adair (1983)—focusing on team performance gives managers and supervisors another way to shape performance. Instead of correcting individual performance based on threat of termination, it can be corrected based on the risk of letting the team down.

Even advertising can have an impact on team spirit, as evidenced in the famous worldwide slogan of Avis: "We try harder.", which delivers a strong message about team spirit. At the same time it promotes pride and makes employees want to live up to its message.

PERFORMANCE STANDARDS

Performance standards must be constructed in such a way that they inspire exceptional performance rather than demand standard performance. On a British Airways flight, the performance standard is to serve customers so that they are satisfied, which includes volunteering to give a cup of coffee to a passenger who has been asleep on a long flight even though it is close to landing time. In contrast, on Lufthansa, the performance standard is to serve coffee at specified times. A passenger awakening under the same conditions who asks for a cup of coffee is not permitted to have one. On British Airways, staff members try to reseat passengers to accommodate smoking preferences; on Lufthansa, staff see that passengers follow the rules.

Performance standards for routine activities are often established based on market research. For example, customers want a fast food meal in two minutes; therefore the performance standard becomes to deliver a fast food meal in two minutes. Performance standards for nonroutine activities are often overlooked, even in recurring situations. The airlines have a performance standard to handle overbooked flights, but car rental companies have no performance standard to handle overbookings when cars are unavailable. Yet performance standards for nonroutine activities are often more important than those for routine situations. First, they give employees confidence that they can satisfy the customer and not be involved in an uncomfortable situation. Second, research by TARP indicates that customers who experience a problem and have it handled well can be more loyal than those who routinely experience ordinary service. Thus, the standards for nonroutine situations can be more important for winning customer loyalty.

POLICIES AND PROCEDURES

Most successful companies operate with policies and procedures to ensure proper accounting, administration, and control. Policies and procedures must also support the delivery of superior service, and striking a proper balance is often difficult.

At Avis in Europe, customers had been allowed to pay their car rental bills using two different charge cards or credit cards. Some tourists found it useful, at the end of a trip, to be able to split their bill, for example, between a MasterCard and a Visa Card. When the Wizard of Avis computer system was implemented in 1985, the system did not allow this feature. Programming the system to allow payment with two or three different credit cards was investigated, but it would have been costly and would have resulted in a delay to the total implementation of a system that offered customers many other benefits. There were no data readily available on the numbers of customers who wanted to pay with two or three credit cards or, more importantly, on how many customers would be lost if this feature were discontinued. Without data about customer satisfaction to offset the cost of changing the system, Avis made the only decision possible to give maximum benefit to the widest base of customers—implement Wizard without this feature.

Customers are both demanding and understanding. They expect service for their money, but are also willing to pay a premium price for premium service, generally understanding that companies have to make a profit. There are, of course, a small percentage of customers who make unreasonable demands, and a company has to be willing to make a cost-based decision on whether to keep these customers.

Policies and procedures must support a company's commitment to superior service delivery and also provide proper controls. Also, the policies and procedures in service delivery functions and in service support functions must support each other. Everyone knows of instances in which service delivery or customer contact personnel quoted one price and the bill came later with another price or in which the product or service promised turned out to be quite different from the created expectation. These discrepancies disappoint customers and damage business. Policies and procedures throughout an organization need to support the overall goals and service strategy.

CONCEPTUAL SKILLS

Many companies have built their fortunes on the strict control and development of employees' technical skills—the consistent quality and delivery of a Big Mac, the punctuality of a Lufthansa flight, the standard furnishings and service offerings of a Holiday Inn, the performance of an IBM computer terminal. Service-oriented companies have begun to build further based on control and development of employees' behavioral skills: the friendly "down-home" greeting of a waitress in a New Jersey diner, the "have a nice day" and "thank you for calling us" closings of an agent in a centralized reservation office, the promise of a room service breakfast on time from a Marriott hotel, the service agreements offered on an Ericsson computer terminal. Companies have made great strides in this area, and customer expectations have begun to rise.

It is clear that rising customer expectations leads to rising standards of service. The marketplace forces companies to improve or lose market share. Leaders that emerge are those that can develop the conceptual skills of their employees: to see how one's job relates to the overall goals and service strategy of the company or organization and to intuitively use technical and behavioral skills to create measurable and profitable customer satisfaction.

At Bowler's Grocery Store in Bray, England, Stan and Elsie Bowler and their staff create measurable and profitable customer satisfaction each day. At one time the store had not been run by the Bowlers, when they sold the tiny grocery store, depended upon by the village's five-thousand inhabitants, but the new owners were unsuccessful and the Bowlers returned by popular demand. The same grocery items are available in large modern supermarkets, understandably at a lower price. The store is in small quarters, making it hard for customers to shop in comfort and for the staff to keep shelves stocked and customers served. There is no standard for waiting time—on a busy Saturday morning, a customer might have to wait 20 minutes at the tiny meat counter and another 20 minutes to tally the items and pay the bill. There are no performance guarantees—a customer might have to come back after the vegetable and fruit delivery to get a common vegetable or might have to wait until the next week for a certain bottle of wine. But if sour cream isn't available, one of the staff will be glad to explain how to make sour cream from items available in the shop. The service strategy is quite simply to serve customers until they're satisfied. In this tiny shop, customers have had all their grocery and wine orders filled, and gotten directions to private homes in the area, advice on how to find a gardener, well-cleaned Thanksgiving turkeys at the appropriate time, delivery service to the home, advice on community activities, pleasant conversation, and the weather report.

Many will argue that small independent businesses are the only businesses able to give this service. But this is the challenge that faces the large enterprises of today and tomorrow. Placing trust in employees to exercise their skills in the pursuit of the service strategy—giving them training, flexible policies and procedures, a clear understanding of job duties and challenging performance standards, and opportunity—has a price. And that price must be compared with the revenues and profits that come from satisfied customers. Too often the price of trusting employees, of paying for mistakes and dishonesties, has been looked at in isolation, as a mere number. That number needs to be seen together with its balancing partners—the exceptional feats of service that may cement a customer's relationship with a service provider for life, the small extra touches that keep customers coming back, the brief interludes of pleasure that occur between employee and customer when service has been provided and received.

EMPOWERMENT

In line with developing the conceptual skills and trusting service delivery employees is empowerment—giving them the power to deliver customer satisfaction in accordance with the company's service strategy.

Empowerment is being used by exceptional service companies to increase measured levels of customer satisfaction, to reduce the cost of complaint handling at headquarters, and to encourage exceptional employee performance. Empowerment gives service delivery employees the necessary tools and authority to resolve on the spot most or all problems or questions with customers, eliminating the need for a customer to complain to headquarters and reducing the number of dissatisfied customers who will not complain but simply switch brands.

The most practical way to establish and provide appropriate tools and authority levels is to talk to service delivery employees. Experience in many companies shows that service delivery employees generally ask for less than management originally thought they might need. In fact, TARP's work with companies has led them to conclude that the top managers are more inclined to overspend than are front-line service delivery employees.

Equipping employees with the tools and ensuring proper controls on authority levels have proved to be simple tasks for most companies. Some of the tools used by the centralized customer service department at a headquarters office might have to be spread out to service delivery points and proper controls and procedures developed. Additional training and guidelines may have to be given to service delivery personnel and their supervisors or managers. Also, a reporting mechanism or system may need to be initiated so that results can be measured and reported.

Being able to solve problems as they happen gives service delivery employees ongoing opportunities to deliver superior service. Trust is motivational; the reduced risk of unpleasant confrontations with customers is encouraging. In addition, a company reduces the risk of unhappy customers simply taking their business elsewhere. Most companies have found that empowering the front-line saves money in the centralized customer service department because it reduces the number of complaints received. TARP has also found escalation to be important: disgruntled customers who harbor their complaints until they get time to write or call the company's headquarters office intensify and embellish the complaint, making it more costly to handle and allowing time for dangerous word-of-mouth advertising.

COMPLIMENTS

That even a few words in this book need to address compliments—verbal or written compliments from customers about service—is in itself an indictment of the service industry. But many companies do not have an organized, ongoing method for routing compliments back to employees, particularly geographically widespread organizations in which a compliment is received in Singapore about service delivered by employees in Tulsa or Paris.

Verbal compliments should be recorded: the format is not important. Verbal and written compliments should be passed on to all of the employees or teams of employees who participated in or contributed to the compliment and to their immediate supervisors or managers. This should be done regularly at all times, not just as a seasonal or one-month program, so that employees can look forward to it. These requirements are the bare essentials.

Compliments, however, provide a much broader opportunity to increase motivation. Many companies feature compliments and the involved employees in house organs and internal communications. Some companies send the compliment to the employee along with a personal note of thanks from the chief executive or a senior executive. Some even send a certificate or a monetary reward or include compliments in incentive programs. The amount of effort and money spent on using compliments to motivate and encourage superior performance is generally returned many times over, although it may be difficult to measure.

Some caution should be exercised in designing reward programs so that employees are not encouraged to beg customers for compliments. Also, front-line service delivery supervisors and managers should see that customers who have complimented employees do not receive excessive attention, to the detriment of other customers.

INCENTIVES

The use of incentives often produces an interesting dilemma for a company. There is no doubt that an incentive program—economic reward of some type for desired performance—brings about the desired performance. But if the desired performance is a regular part of the job, the incentive should be a permanent feature of salary and compensation. The temptation to use an incentive program is particularly strong when a new service performance is being introduced. If the service will become a permanent part of routine performance, then the incentive program may have to become a permanent feature.

Some companies compensate solely by incentive programs; others use incentives to supplement a small base salary. Still others offer incentives as a permanent feature, giving additional salary for exceptional performance or offering points toward gifts.

Incentives must be fair, and it may be difficult to measure service performance. Quality assurance visits, customer comment cards, customer satisfaction tracking systems, and complaints and compliments provide such measures. For temporary incentives, temporary measurements can be used, such as the staff compliment cards carried by Avis corporate customers in the United States to give to Avis employees or the thank you cards given to British Airways Executive Club members to reward British Airways staff. Incentive plans should be announced to employees before the plans begin, with complete explanations of rules and rewards.

As with programs rewarding compliments, incentive programs should be designed so that employees are not encouraged to beg customers to accept or buy something. Also, front-line service delivery supervisors and managers must see that customers who frequently purchase incentivized products or services do not receive excessive attention to the detriment of other customers. In the car rental industry over the years, many incentives have been run on sales of collision damage waiver and personal accident insurance, resulting in customers feeling they were misled or forced into purchasing these options.

REWARDS AND RECOGNITION

In the summer season, the windows of every hotel and home in the Tirol section of Austria teem with brilliantly colored flowers in window boxes. Some are so brilliant and perfect—even those displayed from dilapidated older buildings or from farm houses—that a tourist is often tempted to ask whether they're real. At the Hotel Klosterbraeu, the chambermaids are responsible for the hotel's flower boxes, and they share the honor and recognition when the hotel wins the village award, as it often does.

Reward and recognition programs can be as varied and numerous as the imagination allows. Many companies use overlapping programs; others change them frequently to maintain interest.

In the service industry tips are the most common customer-driven reward. So are the simple words "thank you" from customer to service employee. Many other reward and recognition schemes are company-driven: employee of the week, station of the month, most improved service facility this year, lowest number of complaints this month, greatest improvement in compliments this quarter, highest ranking team on customer satisfaction tracking system, and the like. The reward or recognition may be anything from a simple wall plaque or lapel pin to an expensive vacation.

What is most important is that superior service is rewarded and recognized—that service improvement is rewarded and recognized —even that *efforts* are rewarded and recognized.

TARP chairman Marc Grainer tells a story about an enthusiastic executive's explanation of the company's rewards for both sales and service. Outstanding sales achievement was rewarded with a color television set; outstanding service achievement was rewarded with a lapel pin. As the executive spoke, he realized that the differing reward values in themselves delivered a strong message to employees.

SERVICE OFFERINGS

In order to continuously create the opportunity for people to deliver superior service, a company must monitor customer response to the products and services it offers. While this is generally in the realm of the marketing department, service delivery and service support personnel can often give valuable information on what customers want and need.

If a company offers all the products and services that customers want, employees feel a sense of pride. When customers often ask for products and services not offered by the company, employees feel frustration and begin to lower their opinion of what they do offer. Temporary shortages of products and services can also strain employees if they happen too often. Occasional shortages may create opportunities for employees to think of superior service alternatives.

CUSTOMER EDUCATION

The need for customer education may impede the delivery of superior service. If service delivery employees have to recite the same instructions to customers time and time again or if most customers are confused by what they have to do, customer education may be needed to clear the way for employees to deliver superior service.

A common example is a situation in which service lines are not well defined, resulting in customers being in the wrong line or being served out of turn. Customers become annoyed, and employees feel harassed as the opportunity to deliver superior service fades.

Customer education is easily handled in some of these situations by directional or informational signs and leaflets to put customers in the right place and doing the right things to obtain the service they want.

GUIDELINES FOR CHIEF EXECUTIVES

Sigi Seyrling creates the opportunity for people to deliver superior service by providing staff in the Siglu bar sufficient to meet its service strategy. Sir Colin Marshall began the long process of turning service around at British Airways by reducing staff, yet he creates opportunities for people to deliver superior service through team spirit, recognition, empowerment, service offerings, and a wide range of other tactics. Jan Carlzon used the inverted pyramid structure to create more opportunity and empowerment for the customer contact personnel at SAS.

The methods for creating opportunity are many and varied, and often not decisions of chief executives. The decisions at lower levels, however, are influenced by the chief executive's management style and expressed commitment to superior service.

Chief executives should consider the following:

1. Do I approve staffing levels in support of my company's service strategy and against customer satisfaction levels rather than just on productivity statistics?

2. Do I feel I have a team working with me to achieve common goals?

3. Do I request progress reports on the development of the conceptual skills of my company's employees in addition to progress reports on the development of technical and behavioral skills?

4. Do my company's service delivery employees have the tools and authority levels to deliver superior service in all situations?

5. Do I or my senior executives personally become involved in rewards, recognition, and compliments?

6. Does my company offer the products and services customers want?

7. What decisions and actions have I taken in the last year to create the opportunity for people to deliver superior service?

GUIDELINES FOR FRONT-LINE SERVICE DELIVERY PERSONNEL

At Bollom's Dry Cleaning Service in Bracknell, England, front-line service delivery personnel follow rigid rules and regulations, refusing to accept garments until the customer has washed off excessive dirt, demanding that customers give complete details of any spots, forcing customers to sign a waiver of responsibility for unusual garments and uncommon fabrics. Tied down in this way, front-line service delivery personnel find it hard to satisfy customers and deliver superior service.

If they work in places like Bollom's, front-line service delivery personnel feel they can do little to deliver superior service. They must follow the rules to keep their jobs and build their chances for promotion. But they can look for any chances, however small, to move the company or organization in the right direction.

At a medium-volume Avis rental station, customers with confirmed reservations for luggage racks repeatedly experienced dissatisfaction, for this feature was available on only one car model. They complained to the station manager, whose office overlooks the rental desk, but there was little he could do. Several times the station manager went to his boss to recommend that either Avis purchase luggage racks or that Avis worldwide reservation offices show the luggage racks as unavailable at this station so that customers could not reserve them. The requests were refused: luggage racks cost money, and customers might reserve with competitors if Avis didn't offer them. When his boss went on vacation, the station manager checked the approval and purchasing authority he had while in charge and purchased luggage racks right up to this limit.

Risk-taking can result in termination of employment, and it is not recommended that employees take broad risks to satisfy customers in conflict with company rules, regulations, and decisions. However, front-line service delivery personnel should support all of the company's opportunities for superior service delivery and consider the following:

1. Do I always try to work as part of a team and contribute to team spirit?

2. Do I perform my job in line with its performance standards and within its policies and procedures?

3. Do I think about the contact I have with customers, how well each contact satisfies customers, and how this fits with my company's overall goals and service strategy?

4. Do I make suggestions through proper channels, such as employee surveys, to improve my opportunities to deliver superior service?

5. Do I know the tools and level of authority I have to deliver superior service, and do I exercise them to the fullest extent?

6. Do I accept compliments graciously, both directly from customers and through company channels?

7. Do I actively participate in reward and recognition programs run by my company?

8. Do I pass on through appropriate channels my ideas for service offerings that my customers seem to want?

9. Do I pass on through appropriate channels my ideas for necessary customer education?

10. Do I seize each and every opportunity to deliver superior service to my customers?

GUIDELINES FOR BACK-OFFICE SERVICE SUPPORT PERSONNEL

Back-office service support personnel, like front-line service delivery personnel, are not often in a position to change company direction, but they enable front-line service delivery personnel to deliver superior service.

The kitchen staff who cleans the dishes and prepares and arranges the food in a restaurant gives the waiters and waitresses the opportunity to provide superior service. The insurance clerks who process claims forms for customers with speed and efficiency enable the claims representatives to deliver superior service. The charge card clerks who enter data and create charge cards enable the charge card sales representative to deliver superior service. These are but a few of many examples. Back-office service support personnel *can* deliver superior service; for example, the tailor who stays late to alter a customer's garment, the mail room employees who work through their lunch break to get a customer's order shipped out immediately, and the technicians who carefully double-check a piece of electronic equipment before it is delivered.

Back-office service support personnel should consider the following:

1. Do I always try to work as part of a team and contribute to team spirit?

2. Do I perform my job to the best of my ability in support of service delivery to customers?

3. Do I make suggestions through proper channels, such as employee surveys, to improve my opportunities to support superior service delivery?

4. Do I accept compliments graciously?

5. Do I actively participate in reward and recognition programs run by my company?

GUIDELINES FOR MIDDLE MANAGEMENT

Middle managers assess and put forth staffing recommendations, determine detailed performance standards, create specific policies and procedures, develop the conceptual skills of their employees, provide tools and approve levels of authority for service delivery, design and put forward reward, incentive, and recognition programs, and create team spirit. Middle managers may also block programs and opportunities for superior service delivery without the knowledge of senior executives.

In *In Search of Excellence* (1982), Thomas J. Peters and Robert H. Waterman, Jr., describe the zeal and commitment of Frito-Lay's nearly ten thousand-person sales force and its "99.5 percent service level," which causes Frito-Lay to "spend several hundred dollars sending a truck to restock a store with a couple of $30 cartons of potato chips." While it would be an analyst's dream to cut costs at Frito-Lay, "Frito management, looking at market shares and margins, won't tamper with the zeal of the sales force."

Middle managers must look at their specific job function and at overall company goals and consider the following:

1. Do I understand my company's service strategy and the role I and my team play in it?

2. Do I actively promote team spirit?

3. Do the policies and procedures within my area support the service strategy?

4. Do I devote time to explaining decisions to my staff and sending them on training programs in order to develop their conceptual skills?

5. Do my employees have the right tools and levels of authority to carry out their jobs in line with my company's service strategy?

6. Do I regularly review the programs in my area for rewarding and recognizing employees?

7. Do I listen to employee ideas about service offerings and customer education in my area of responsibility and ensure they are carried forward?

8. Do I do everything within my power to always create opportunities for people to deliver superior service?

9

Advertise and Sell Service, and Stand Behind It

In 1962, the Doyle, Dane, Bernbach advertising agency was charged with devising an ad campaign for the nation's number two car rental company, Avis-Rent-A-Car. Stuck for an idea, they did some research, including visiting some Avis stations and the stations of its competitors. Their conclusions were not inspiring. Avis offered basically the same cars as its competitors. Despite the best efforts of car rental marketing and senior management and of numerous ad agencies, the rates for renting a car were basically the same. Even the networks of locations were comparable. But, there was just one small area where the Doyle, Dane, Bernbach people believed they saw a difference. It was in the spirit of the Avis employees. And so was born Avis's famous advertising slogan, "We try harder.", a slogan that not only described the spirit of Avis employees but that helped to shape the attitudes of new employees joining the company. And, of course, it brought customers to Avis.

ADVERTISING SERVICE

Standard advertising textbooks say that the three functions of advertising are to inform, to persuade, and to remind the audience known as customers or consumers. William R. George and Leonard L. Berry, in "Guidelines for the Advertising of Services," in Christopher H. Lovelock's *Services Marketing* (1984), provide six guidelines for advertising services, as opposed to goods, based on some of the special characteristics of services. The first guideline is about advertising that has a positive impact on customer contact employees. "When the performances of people are what customers buy, the advertiser needs to be concerned, not only with encouraging customers to buy, but also with encouraging employees to perform."

Advertising has an impact on employees who see it directly or hear about it from customers. Yet too often, the creative discussions center only on the traditional role of advertising: getting customers to buy. The attitude is, if the advertising happens to have an impact on employees, that's fine, but surely it's a minor consideration in the overall scheme. Negative examples, such as National Airlines' "Fly Me, I'm Nancy," several years ago, reinforce the point that strong positive advertising that hints at or features the skills of employees has a measurable positive impact on employee performance. Robin Davies, vice president of sales and marketing for Hertz in Europe, Africa, and the Middle East and himself a former Avis employee, speaking at the Business Travel Forum in London in 1987, said, with a nostalgic look in his eyes, "I've always thought Avis had a bit of an advantage over us with their advertising slogan."

Effectively advertising a service means showing it so that the service can be understood by potential customers. While it is easy to show a product—and a customer happily using it—some services are not easily illustrated. Showing a luxurious hotel interior can imply that luxury service is given there; showing smiling, attentive service delivery employees performing a service for a customer can portray one aspect of service, in many industries. But finding an image that portrays the services given by an insurance company, a financial services firm, or a law firm can be difficult. Advertising services like these generally involve translating a range of services into a symbol to which customers can relate. Leonard L. Berry, in "Services Marketing Is Different," in Christopher H. Lovelock's, *Services Marketing* (1984), asks readers to consider the following:

"'You're in good hands with Allstate.'

'I've got a piece of the rock.'

'Under the Traveler's umbrella.'

'The Nationwide blanket of protection.'

"Hands, rocks, umbrellas, and blankets are used to more effectively communicate what insurance can provide people: they are devices used to make the service more easily grasped mentally."

Time Manager International's "Putting People First" training program divides services into two main types—material service and personal service. Material service consists of price, quantity, quality, and timing, and is the easier to define, measure, and compare. Material service is the speed with which a rental car is delivered, the timeliness of an airline flight, the repair that is done when promised. Personal service refers to the human interaction that takes place as material service is being provided. Personal service is what the sales clerk says to a customer who is returning a faulty item, how friendly the waiter or waitress is when serving a customer, what the insurance sales representative says and how he or she says it.

Service advertising frequently features the material service, guaranteeing customers the lowest price in town, the fastest service in the field, the highest quality in physical comfort. This approach takes two key risks. One is that material service can be duplicated by competitors or that the perception of providing the same or even better material service can be created in competitors' advertising campaigns. If one company advertises that it can deliver room service breakfasts within 15 minutes of the order time, another company can advertise that it delivers room service breakfasts within 10 minutes of the order time. The second is that while dissatisfied customers most often complain about material service failures, it is often the personal service failures that made the reaction strong enough to generate a complaint. Stated another way, if personal service is good enough, customers will not complain about material service failures. A frequent guest at the Sheraton Skyline Hotel in Tulsa, Oklahoma, tolerated small service failures at the hotel, such as waiting too long for the bill in the coffee shop and missing two telephone messages, because the staff was always so nice to her, recognizing her as a frequent guest and calling her by name. However, when she found a field mouse in her room, she went to the front desk to complain. "That's okay," said the front desk clerk, who knew her, "We won't charge you for the extra guest in the room this time." She couldn't help but laugh, knowing the staff would take care of the problem.

Personal service often causes customers to choose one brand over another, yet many service companies are afraid to advertise personal service. In some industries, differences in personal service may be the only distinguishing feature, advantage, or benefit between brands. It's the reason why many residents of England frequent their "local" pub, the one that gives them friendly, personal service. Advertising personal service, such as British Airways has done in 1987 and 1988 with its emphasis on caring for people, has a double effect, persuading customers to try the service and prodding employees to live up to what is advertised.

Companies may be reluctant to advertise that a company or organization has solutions for service or product failures. It calls attention to the reality that products or services fail, that photocopy machines break down, that overbookings may occur, that staff may not always be friendly and unrushed. Yet customers are often well aware of these problems, either from personal experience or word-of-mouth advertising from their friends. Knowing that a company has solutions to these problems creates customer confidence, both in the company's dedication to preventing the problem from occurring routinely and in the company's commitment to delivering a helpful solution when the problem does occur. To put this into advertising is a bold step but one that has won customers and market shares for those who have done it. When customers know that they will be looked after when problems occur, or that they will receive continuing service on a major item, the assurance increases their intent to purchase that product or service again.

ADVERTISING AIMS

A company advertises to inform, to persuade, and to remind. To advertise one has to decide what the message will be, to whom it should be told (the audience), how it should be told, and where to tell it. These decisions affect the outcome or return on investment —the customers who come to buy the product or service because of advertising and the customers who are reminded that they are satisfied with the product or service and can buy again.

Harvey R. Cook, in his book for small businesses, *Selecting Advertising Media* (1969), states, "The aim of advertising should be to develop customers, not for single sales, but for repeat purchases. Someone has called it manufacturing customers. Few of the products and services we buy during a lifetime are one-time purchases. We tend to buy, on repeat purchases, what has pleased us before, and to buy it where we have been satisfied."

Advertising generates repeat business, as does delivering superior service and satisfying customers. This also means that companies repeatedly face decisions on continuing to spend money on advertising. In many industries, the impact of advertising is difficult to prove with numbers, making the advertising budget a target of cost reduction measures. Equally hard to prove numerically is the impact of temporarily not advertising, until, of course, it begins to show on the revenue line.

In advertising service, continuity is particularly important, for two reasons. One is related to the usual reasons companies continue advertising—to continue to keep the company's name, image, and services in the minds of consumers. The second is specific to service. Because service is often described as intangible and considered difficult to depict, particularly in print advertising, the reminding message must be repeatedly reinforced. In addition, competitors will continue to advertise the benefits of their material and personal service, and one's own message must compete. For service advertising, this message must have a symbol or image of continuity: the "We try harder." slogan that has appeared in all Avis ads since 1962, the rock that has appeared in Prudential's ads in words or pictures for over 20 years, and Frank Perdue himself appearing in his company's ads over many years.

While "advertising" usually connotes television, radio, and print advertising, direct mail advertising has become a major force. In the service industry, the key feature of direct mail advertising is its ability to reach the right target audience. While a television ad may reach many millions, the target audience may be only a portion of this vast audience, and money is being spent to reach more people than necessary.

In the service industry, direct mail advertising is particularly useful to help regain lost customers or to prompt additional business from those customers that appear to have become inactive. Many service companies have invested heavily in marketing data bases to more accurately identify their customers and market segments. These same marketing data bases are used to drive direct mail advertising campaigns aimed at getting inactive customers to buy the product or service again or to provide feedback as to why they are not buying.

Direct mail advertising in many service industries is useful for smoothing out seasonal peaks and valleys by offering special discounts and promotions at certain times of the year. These direct mail campaigns can also be driven by internal marketing data bases or by direct mail lists purchased externally.

Direct mail advertising has one disadvantage that a service company must overcome. Employees are more likely to see television, radio, or print advertising and to hear about it from customers. Unless all employees are placed on "seed lists" to receive direct mail advertising, its potential impact on employees is lost. Even more damaging is a direct mail campaign that makes special offers to customers before service delivery and service support personnel know about them.

SERVICE GUARANTEES

Over the head of the Ramada Inn cashier hung a sign, "Your room free if we fail to ask you for a reservation at your next Ramada destination." Near the gas pumps of a Mobil station hung several signs, "Your tank of gas free if we fail to ask if we can check your oil." At rental counters in Sweden, Interrent displayed signs reading, "Your rental free if we fail to answer your complaint within 24 hours." And there is the sign that has hung in many businesses, "Satisfaction guaranteed, or your money back."

These service guarantees put teeth into service advertising, guaranteeing customers a level of material or personal service with a promise of payment or solution when failures occur. Some service guarantees, as in the Ramada and Mobil examples, guarantee service while being sales tools designed to generate additional revenues —a second Ramada room, a quart of oil—for the company.

Service guarantees, when proposed or considered by a company, inevitably run into objections from cost accountants of how much failures will cost. The same cost accountants are quick to approve an accounting control, such as telephoning for authorization on customers' credit cards for all purchases over $100, often without asking how often employees will fail to follow the procedure. But in that case the procedure saves money for the company, and the cost of a few human errors is tolerable. The same principle needs to be applied to service guarantees. They increase customer satisfaction and reduce complaints; therefore the cost of a few human errors is tolerable.

Service guarantees are a double-edged attack. Advertised, they attract customers and set performance standards for employees. In effect, service guarantees strengthen a performance standard because both the customer and the employee monitor compliance. Yet this may be another point of attack for the cost accountants. They argue that telephone authorizations on credit cards can be controlled by requiring employees to record the authorization number on an auditable document. With service guarantees, there may be only one customer contact employee and one customer alone in an office together, and the words they say to each other will be a matter of one's word versus the other's word. But most customers are reasonable and those that are not would probably end up as a costly complaint at head office anyway.

Service guarantees encourage employees to do the job right the first time. Not doing it right the first time, with or without a service guarantee, costs a company money in correcting the error, in negative word-of-mouth advertising, in handling a letter or call of complaint, or in lost business due to dissatisfaction. The arguments for service guarantees are similar to those for empowerment and preventing escalation because they encourage on-the-spot problem solving.

Of course, good market research and analysis of customer needs must assure that service guarantees promise something customers want. Several years ago, Avis advertising promised customers that if they had a confirmed reservation for a car, the company would do its very best to try to deliver the car. Customers, however, wanted to be *guaranteed* a car when they had a confirmed reservation. Before the ad, many thought a confirmed reservation *was* a guarantee; the ad produced doubt.

Constructing a meaningful service guarantee means checking that it supports the company's service strategy. But a proposed service guarantee, vetted through all the functional areas, may become so diluted that it offers only a minimum standard of performance, one that is easily copied or bettered by competitors, and one that does not inspire exceptional employee performance.

IMAGE AND IDENTITY

In August 1987, Harrod's in London announced its five-year plan to spend 2 million pounds for a facelift to the world-famous store.

That such a store should have a major remodeling is not so meaningful as the way in which it is being done—using marble instead of plastic or plasterboard, using silk instead of hessian wallpaper, tearing down plaster to reveal soaring vaulted ceilings, using experts to uncover a hidden mahogany staircase or to pull down mirrors covering solid marble, in short, restoring the store to its former grandeur. While the owners are giving great importance to restoring the company's once-famed service reputation, they also consider important the lavish spending to restore the physical environment.

The image of the physical environment where service is delivered is important. Along with the material and personal service provided by employees, this environment delivers a strong message to customers about what they can expect.

The image must, however, fit the service strategy of the company, whether it is the clean family image presented by McDonald's, the quiet, efficient, technologically advanced look of the Hershey Medical Center in Pennsylvania, or the marble luxury of Harrod's. Sometimes the image will have to be adjusted to suit local service strategies and local expectations. Service counters in Hawaii—from fruit shops to hotels to car rental companies—create an image associated with the tropical vacation paradise in which they do business. Suburban offices may have to have a more friendly local image to attract local residents as customers than the posh, expensive look of an airport or city center office with international clientele. Many international and national companies have achieved success with a standardized image in line with their service strategy, with service delivery points worldwide being outfitted by a central office fitter in one city.

The image of the physical surroundings works with the image of the people who deliver service or are seen by customers, and that image includes their clothes, personal hygiene habits, and manner of speaking and moving. Health spa personnel graphically illustrate the perfectly toned, beautifully shaped bodies one hopes to achieve by joining. Disney World's emphasis on employees' playing Roles in a daily Show shapes attitudes of prospective applicants about service delivery and creates an image. Instead of following grooming or uniform regulations, Disney World's employees outfit and groom themselves for their roles.

Image and identity, like advertising in general, influence both customers and employees. Employees who work in attractive physical surroundings and wear uniforms they like perform their jobs better, with higher productivity and a higher degree of customer care.

SELLING SERVICE

John Stone, writing in *Business Travel News* (September 7, 1987) about car rental industry focus, reports that Cliff Haley, president of Budget-Rent-A-Car Corporation, "disagreed with his competitors in saying that price, not service, will remain most important to accounts. 'I don't know that you can convince them about service; the differences are in the rates.'"

This statement appeared in the press as IBM in Europe signed an exclusive agreement to rent cars from Avis. While price charts for each country in Europe were included in the contract, the majority of the contract's pages spelled out the material and personal services that Avis offered to provide IBM renters.

Selling service is often considered more difficult than selling a product, and it is clear that many companies are selling their products more successfully by selling service with the product. But some of the obstacles to selling service include:

1. The word *intangible* is often associated with selling service. This forces the marketing and sales people in an organization to carefully devise selling propositions so that customers can understand what is being offered.

2. Because the service being offered may be difficult to describe to customers, the selling propositions can easily promise more than is possible.

3. When the task of proving tangible service selling propositions to customers becomes too difficult, the sales force has a tendency to retreat to selling price.

4. Consistency in quality of service is directly related to the consistency of the quality and skills of the employees delivering and supporting service. The sales force has to rely upon its service delivery and service support colleagues, particularly in industries having heavy reliance on franchising or on widespread decentralized delivery points.

5. Selling frequently makes its strongest case by making comparisons with competitors. While service can be the most powerful distinguishing feature, advantage, and benefit over competitors, it is the most difficult to prove because of the lack of competitive data on service from external recognized, unbiased sources over a period of time. This is particularly true of personal service over material service.

Despite these obstacles, superior service companies sell service rather than price or product, and customers often buy service rather than price or product.

Selling service successfully requires market research into customer needs, service offerings that respond to those needs, and awareness through advertising and promotion. Next are the sales strategy and selling propositions, training for the sales force, and sales aids and tools for the sales force.

Often the sales force is armed with attractive price sheets but not enough materials to help them sell service, or funding has been used for pricing materials at the expense of service selling materials. Just as in advertising, more money or effort may have to be devoted to creating pictures and symbols that demonstrate and prove the service offerings.

Training is important, for service selling propositions differ from company to company just as do product selling propositions. In one service company, the training department fought long and hard to get management to agree to selling skills training for the sales force. Working with a young sales force whose experience was primarily in product selling, the training department carefully translated the service propositions for selling into product packages. Still others worked with the sales department, again developing product packages. The experiment worked well in the pilot course with role plays clearly demonstrating that students could sell service effectively by thinking of each group of services as a product. The experiment was a huge success until the closing minutes when a stray executive stopped by to say hello to the students. He had only a few words to say, "You have to remember you're selling service, not products. And that's more difficult. Good luck!" It took only a few words to ruin a week-long training program.

The role of front-line service delivery personnel in the selling effort is crucial. In many companies they sell service daily and can sell additional services, related services and more of a service. Often, front-line service delivery personnel, being at the lower end of the pay scale, view their company's products and services as beyond their own economic reach and thus show reluctance to actively sell. Good training can give these employees the confidence to proudly sell their company's products and services.

INTERNAL COMMUNICATION AND TRAINING

Advertising and sales are effective only if the company is well prepared to provide that service to customers. And the quality of the service being delivered will only be as good as the quality of the people providing the service (front-line service delivery personnel, back-office service support personnel, and their management).

Employees should be trained in the services they are expected to provide to customers. They need technical skills training to know how to operate computer terminals, to process material services, to follow administrative procedures, and so on. They need behavioral skills training to know what to say to customers and how to say it in line with the company's service strategy. And they need conceptual skills training to know how their jobs fit into the overall goals of the organization. Training enables employees to satisfy customers—to meet or exceed customers' expectations.

Many service companies excel in initial training but fail to establish a good ongoing method for communicating changes and new service offerings to employees. A franchise environment or an environment with many offices spread out geographically is particularly susceptible to this problem. Funding must support continuous internal communication of new and changed service offerings that reaches every employee, even in the most remote location. A good method is to use site managers or supervisors to deliver training or to deliver new information to their own employees. Another method is to use carefully selected employees at each location to deliver training or new information to colleagues. Computer-assisted instruction, daily messages from computer systems, self-instructional programmed learning packages, internal bulletins or news releases, job aids, instructional sheets, and training guides may be used to distribute information and changes. On a larger scale, location meetings or briefings, traveling roadshows, pep rallies, or new service launches may be used to communicate effectively with employees at all levels. Whatever method is used needs to take into account the technical skills, behavioral skills, and conceptual skills that employees will need to know to effectively execute the new service offering or change with customers.

WARRANTIES, GUARANTEES, AND REFUNDS

Another important aspect of service is standing behind the product. Service guarantees are one way to stand behind service promises. Other methods include warranties and guarantees, which have usually been associated with products. But superior service companies now use warranties and guarantees to back up promises of service.

The most common type of warranty is the one that comes with a new car. Many people associate warranties with lengthy waits for repairs caused by dealers and workshops taking care of "paying customers" first. Many companies, including Toyota, General Motors, and Ford, are now analyzing the impact of customer satisfaction with warranty repairs and how it affects the intent of customers to purchase another car from the manufacturer.

In Sweden, Philipson, importer of Mercedes and Nissan automobiles and owner of the Avis franchise, has made major new initiatives to inject the Avis "We try harder." spirit into its dealerships and workshops, having purchased the Avis franchise with this purpose in mind. For warranty and workshop repairs on Mercedes and Nissan automobiles, Philipson basically has a monopoly, yet the company conducts customer satisfaction research by telephone and is analyzing the intention of Mercedes and Nissan owners to purchase these automobiles again as it is affected by the warranty and repair service given.

At the Chanel boutique in London, Chanel strives for 100 percent customer satisfaction. A customer who paid 400 pounds for a leather briefcase used it once, and the handle broke. The defective briefcase was promptly taken back by Chanel staff with a profuse apology. Attempts were made to find another like it in the shop. That having failed, the briefcase was promptly repaired and mailed free of charge to the customer's home. Chanel staff followed up with a telephone call to see that the customer had received it and was satisfied.

GUIDELINES FOR CHIEF EXECUTIVES

Chief executives often must become directly involved in the company's advertising and sales efforts by approving the actual appearance and message of a major television advertising campaign (or possibly even by appearing in it), approving capital expenditures for image and identity upgrades or changes, and being personally involved in signing up major accounts. Chief executives often have major responsibility for shaping the company's service strategy, either deliberately or indirectly through their actions and decisions, and that strategy will be communicated to customers through the advertising message and the selling propositions.

To move a company to service excellence and keep it there, chief executives need to ask themselves the following:

1. Do my company's advertising messages communicate well the services my company has to offer and are these messages communicated to customers, employees, and owners?

2. Do my company's image and identity programs result in the communication of my company's service strategy effectively to customers, employees, and owners?

3. Does my company actively and effectively sell the services it has to offer?

4. Does my company stand behind its service strategy and the services it provides?

GUIDELINES FOR FRONT-LINE SERVICE DELIVERY PERSONNEL

Front-line service delivery positions are an important part of a company's advertising message and sales effort. Everything these employees say and do in front of customers, even the way they look, communicates with customers about the company and its services.

As vital employees in the company's ability to advertise and sell service and stand behind it, service delivery employees need to ask themselves:

1. Do I do everything within my power to live up to my company's advertising slogans and service guarantees?

2. Do I wear a company-provided uniform with pride?

3. Do I ensure that my personal appearance always conveys the message that I am ready to deliver my company's services to customers?

4. Do I believe in the services my company offers and can I sell them effectively?

5. Do I treat each customer as an individual, try to identify his or her individual needs, and offer all of the products and services that might satisfy these needs?

6. Do I take responsibility for reading all training materials or information announcements about new service offerings or changes carefully and for making sure I understand the services I am expected to offer to customers?

7. Do I know how my company stands behind the service it offers and what my duties are in this process?

8. Do I advertise and sell my company's services outside of my working hours?

GUIDELINES FOR BACK-OFFICE SERVICE SUPPORT PERSONNEL

Because the service that customers receive is a product of what both front-line service delivery and back-office service support personnel do, back-office service support personnel are no less crucial to a company's ability to advertise and sell service, and stand behind it. However, back-office service support personnel are rarely seen by customers. The dish they wash, the tray they prepare, the rental car they service, the warranty repair they make, the baggage they unload, or the bill they send to a customer may make the difference in the service the company is able to advertise, sell, and guarantee to customers.

Back-office service support personnel need to ask themselves:

1. Do I perform each of my job duties to the best of my ability so that advertising and sales promises are kept?

2. Do I believe in the services my company offers?

3. Do I take responsibility for reading all training materials or information announcements that affect my job so that I am able to effectively support new service offerings and changes?

4. Do I know how my company stands behind the service it offers and what my duties are in this process?

5. Do I support my service delivery colleagues in meeting or exceeding customers' expectations?

GUIDELINES FOR MIDDLE MANAGEMENT

In the middle management core of a company most advertising briefs are hammered out, market research is commissioned, sales strategy is formulated, selling propositions are created and trained, capital expenditure requests for office facilities and uniforms are constructed, internal communication and training are developed, and policies and procedures on warranties, guarantees, and refunds are devised.

Middle managers work directly in marketing, advertising, image and identity, training, and sales, and deal daily with these topics. Middle managers should consider the following:

1. Do I do everything within my power to live up to my company's advertising slogans and service guarantees? Do I manage my staff toward the same goal?

2. Do I believe in the services my company offers, and can I sell them effectively?

3. Do I take responsibility for informing my staff about changes and new service offerings so that they may do their jobs effectively?

4. Do I know how my company stands behind the service it offers and what my duties and the duties of my staff are in this process?

5. Do I advertise and sell my company's services outside of my working hours?

6. Do I support front-line service delivery and back-office service support employees in meeting or exceeding customers' expectations?

10

Be Ready to Do Handsprings to Resolve Each Perceived Service Failure

Dear Ms. Lash,
Full marks to Avis—you've proved you do try harder.
I thank you for your prompt, courteous, and constructive reply. . . .
You've kept me in the fold and I will book my Zurich hire in May through Avis. . . .

John K. Dunstan
Managing Director

Dear Ms. Lash,
. . . If you ever pass this way please give us a call and we will take you to lunch in reciprocation. John and I, as marketing people, both know how rare such consumer empathy is.

Susan K. Dunstan
Director

Dear Ms. Lash,

Thank you for your letter of 30th April. I appreciate your candid comments and as you will realize, my main concern was to ensure that the failure in your procedures would be put right at the appropriate level. As this has now been done, this is the end of the matter so far as I am concerned.

Thank you for kindly sending me a customer service certificate for 50 U.S. dollars for my next car rental, which I accept with much pleasure although I must say the possibility of such a gift had not been in my mind when writing!

Peter F. Earlam
Chairman

For the attention of Linda M. Lash, Director of Marketing,

. . . I also must admit that your consideration for the service given to me has given me reason to look at my ethics as a customer. Occasionally I will in future use the services of Avis and again compare Avis service with others. . . .

Finally, if you are able to bring all members of the Avis staff to adopt your spirit of fair business Avis will be an outstanding company— and I'm sure you will try.

Eskil Naeslund

Dear Ms. Lash:

Thank you very much for your exceptionally prompt and responsive letter of 30 April. You have completely restored my faith in Avis and I have already booked Avis cars for my next two trips. . . .

Stephen H. Caine
President

These letters were unsolicited, and they are quite different from each writer's original letter of complaint.

The service industry offers ample opportunity for things to go wrong, and things *do* go wrong. What distinguishes exceptional service companies from others is the actions they take with a customer when a problem occurs. The most overwhelming reason to take action in this event is purely and simply to get the customer to purchase the product or service again. And in each of the previous excerpts from letters received by the director of marketing at Avis, there is an openly stated or clearly implied intent to purchase the service again.

REPEAT BUSINESS

The paramount reason for a company or organization to spend money on resources to handle complaints and inquiries is to get repeat business. Repeat business generates revenue and profit and turns what is typically viewed as a cost center into a revenue-generating and profit-generating business activity.

A customer who experiences a problem is not necessarily a lost customer. The excellent service companies view the customer with a problem as an opportunity. TARP's research and experience suggests that the customer with a problem is a golden opportunity for a service-obsessed company to demonstrate its commitment and bring the customer back into the fold.

TARP's research also shows that sometimes the customer with a problem is wrong and that it is not the size of the remedy—"giving away the store"—that satisfies the customer but rather the promptness, responsiveness, and clarity of the actions taken and explanations given to the customer.

Many companies operate a centralized customer service department to receive and handle customer complaints and inquiries. Often the performance measures for these departments consist solely of productivity measures: number of complaints handled per representative, number of complaints this month versus last month, number of complaints as a percentage of the company's transactions or sales, cost per complaint, cost per remedy, and so on. These numbers are functional in the daily management of a customer service department. But more important is whether customers will purchase the product or service again as a result of the way their complaint or inquiry was handled. Getting repeat business is the purpose of the customer service department.

COMPLAINTS VERSUS INQUIRIES

Complaints and inquiries are often tracked, counted, and handled separately. But how angry must an inquiry become before it's a complaint, and how mild must a complaint become before it's an inquiry? Some companies have elaborate procedures to distinguish between the two. For example, if it takes longer than ten minutes for a customer service representative to handle an inquiry, it's counted as a complaint.

Customers are not always sure whether they have an inquiry or a complaint, but they know they need something. If a customer has charged a car rental to his American Express account and is contacting the car rental company for a copy of the rental agreement, is he doing it because he is horrified at the total charge (a possible complaint) or because he simply lost his copy and needs it for expense accounting (a possible inquiry)? Will he tell the customer service representative which it is?

Some customers initially voice complaints as inquiries, out of politeness, out of a true need for information (after which they may be satisfied or turn into a complaint), or out of reluctance to "make a scene."

Whether viewed as a complaint or an inquiry, a customer's request for assistance is an opportunity to educate him and to take whatever actions are necessary to cause him to purchase a product or service again.

WORD-OF-MOUTH ADVERTISING

In the service industry, word-of-mouth advertising has come to be recognized as a potent force. Before buying a product, it is easy to go and look at it or ask the opinion of friends and relatives who have used the product. But judging service usually requires first-hand experience. So the experiences of friends and relatives, for example, must be relied upon to find a dentist in a strange city, to find a good dry cleaning service in a new neighborhood, to recommend a hotel or restaurant, to provide the name of an insurance agent, a gardener, a maid.

People tell other people about their experiences—both good and bad—and people ask each other about their experiences. In fact, TARP's research shows that in several industries dissatisfied customers tell twice as many people as do satisfied customers. A company with many dissatisfied customers, particularly those who do not write or call the company to complain, can watch millions of dollars spent in advertising offset by negative word-of-mouth advertising.

TARP uses a formula that combines research on a company's satisfied and dissatisfied customers, the word-of-mouth advertising they generate, and their intent to purchase the product or service again to arrive at the market damage or lost business that results from not satisfying customers. The numbers generated by this formula attract the attention of management to an area that might previously have been viewed as a necessary evil or a cost center.

COMPLAINANT SATISFACTION TRACKING

Few customers who have complained to a company will write back to describe their satisfaction with the way their complaints were handled and state their intentions to purchase the product or service again, as writers of the letters quoted at the beginning of this chapter did. Yet this information is exactly what is needed to measure the success of a company's complaint and inquiry handling methods.

TARP recommends a complainant satisfaction tracking system, also called an inquiry satisfaction tracking system, whereby a sample of customers who have complained or made an inquiry receive postage-paid reply postcards for evaluating the way their complaints were handled in areas such as promptness of response, clarity of response, and general responsiveness to the complaint or inquiry. Customers are also asked whether they intend to purchase the product or service again. The responses can be tabulated by a centralized customer service department, by individual customer service representatives, by field locations, by product, or by teams of complaint and inquiry handling personnel spread through the company. This is an inexpensive way to measure the success of a company's complaint and inquiry handling methods, and it also delivers a strong message to customers about a company's commitment to "do handsprings" to resolve each perceived service failure.

Some industries give complaining or inquiring customers discount coupons or money-off coupons for the next purchase, incorporating a tracking mechanism so that the customer service department will know when the coupons have been used. A problem with this method is that customers will lose or forget coupons but purchase the product or service again. Some method must be developed to accurately measure the success rate in terms of repeat business.

LOYALTY

TARP's research suggests that even more loyal than a customer satisfied by ordinarily good service is a customer who has experienced a problem and received a response equal to or better than expectations. A customer service department, in this role, is an arm of the marketing department for generating brand loyalty.

If a marketing department spends 3 percent of revenues to get new customers, the average revenue per purchase is $100, and an average customer makes six purchases over the next two years, how much will the customer service department spend to respond to a customer's complaint? If customers are complaining and the remedies each cost $10, this money is far better spent to keep the loyalty of existing customers than spending $18 to get new customers. However, if the customer demands a $500 remedy and will accept nothing less, the profit impact must be considered in deciding whether to satisfy this customer.

Loyal customers generate repeat business and positive word-of-mouth advertising. Thus, they have an economic value to the company. Getting new customers is expensive, and marketing and sales people cannot be bringing new customers through the front door while the complaint and inquiry handling personnel lose them out the back door.

PROBLEM SOLVING

The second reason a company spends money on resources to handle complaints and inquiries from customers is to find out what problems are occurring and take preventive action for the future.

One company's audit report showed that a major account had called each month for the last sixteen months to report billing errors. The bills were wrong each month for exactly the same reason, and the company happily altered all sixteen bills. The errors were caused by an incorrect entry in a computer data base. Fixing it required less than 60 seconds of effort by a department in an office less than 50 feet away.

Customer service departments may be staffed by knowledgeable employees who could often pinpoint the company's problem spots. Many of them could also give solutions to the problems—and they'd even be right. But having this knowledge does little good if it doesn't get to the people who fix problems.

Customer service department reports must solve problems, not just categorize complaints and inquiries in a way that has meaning for them but is not actionable by other managers and executives with the authority to fix problems. In such reports it is not uncommon to find the heading "billing error." Only if there is but one type of billing error and one manager in the company who can control it does this heading lead to a solution.

The customer service department must communicate problems to the people in the organization who can solve them, prevent their recurrence, or take the responsibility for allowing them to continue. Whether communication is done by the audit department, in carefully categorized reports with actionable headings from the customer service department to the appropriate managers, in photocopies or individual reports of each complaint sent to the appropriate managers, or any other method, it must be done.

Not all problems can be solved or prevented. Said another way, it may be more cost-effective for a company to allow a problem to continue than to fix it. TARP's market damage economic model provides one way for companies to make this decision. Overbookings in the travel industry are a common example. Despite sophisticated computer systems and policies, overbooking does occur, and most companies in the travel industry have an established remedy. The overbooking problem is not permanently solved because the cost of the solution outweighs the cost of remedies and lost business. But because it may affect repeat business, not fixing a problem should be a carefully weighed decision and not simply the result of poor reporting by the customer service department.

One of the dangers of having a centralized customer service department is that it may handle mistakes rather than reporting them to individual employees for action. Most employees want to do a good job, and they need to know their errors. A report that says "you made 10 errors last month" is insufficient feedback. Employees need guidance or remedial training.

PRODUCT FEEDBACK AND SELLING OPPORTUNITIES

Customer complaints and inquiries provide instant feedback about new products and services. While a new product or service may have been carefully test-marketed, things can go wrong during the launch, particularly if services dependent on employee performance are involved.

The customer service department needs to feed this information promptly to the marketing department and possibly to the training department for communication to employees or retraining. During launches of new services, customer service acts as an arm of the marketing department to provide immediate customer response. This is yet another reason why inquiries are as important to count and track as are complaints, for they may signal a need for customer education or employee training.

Companies operating toll-free telephone centers for customer complaints and inquiries have found that these create selling opportunities. The opportunities could be for cross-selling (selling another of the company's products or services based on a question from a customer or on the discussion that occurs while resolving a problem). Or the opportunities may be for outright selling of more business based on the satisfactory resolution of a problem or inquiry. For this reason, many companies employ skilled, experienced staff in their telephone centers and consider the investment to pay off in sales leads.

PREVENTING ESCALATION

In companies with many busy retail outlets and a centralized customer service department at a headquarters office, the tendency is for front-line service delivery personnel to advise customers with complaints or inquiries to contact the customer service department, particularly if the company has an easily reached toll-free telephone center. When they must serve many waiting customers during a peak period, this solution seems to make sense.

But this approach may be disadvantageous to the company. From the time the question or problem arose to the time of the call, the customer has gained time to think. By this time the question may have turned into a problem or the problem may have turned into several problems. Also the customer may engage in negative word-of-mouth advertising before contacting the customer service department. Because the question or problem has been allowed to escalate, the remedy required to satisfy the customer may cost the company more money. Also, it is often more costly to handle a complaint or inquiry at the head office because of the necessary research time. But the greatest risk is that these customers won't bother to complain but will simply generate negative word-of-mouth advertising and take their business elsewhere.

Complaints and inquiries are best resolved when and where they happen, before they breed negative word-of-mouth advertising, before they become costly to resolve, and before they create lost revenue and profit. This seems simple, yet many companies do not resolve complaints and inquiries at the point of sale by raising the following objections:

1. Front-line service delivery personnel are not trained as well to deal with complaining customers as is the customer service department.

2. We'd have inconsistency because we have so many retail outlets.

3. Customers would take advantage of overworked staff during peak periods.

4. Front-line service delivery staff would give away the store.

5. We couldn't possibly give retail outlets the tools to solve service problems on the spot. There's the risk of theft and misuse.

6. It's best not to let other customers hear the complaint.

7. Other customers might overhear the problem's solution and want the same.

8. There's not enough staff to handle it.

These objections point to some of the steps necessary to enable front-line service delivery personnel to resolve complaints and inquiries when they occur. They need training, procedures, guidelines, and tools. Controls are necessary to keep costs in line and simple reporting is necessary for measuring the success of the plan.

Experience in many companies indicates that it takes longer to handle an escalated complaint or inquiry at the head office than at the point of service. This translates into increased staffing. While it is not easy to eliminate one employee at the head office and add one-tenth of an employee to each of 10 service delivery points (and the math is never this easy), the company must find a way to handle complaints and inquiries at service delivery points by rearranging priorities, streamlining administrative tasks, rationalizing job duties, or even justifying additional employees to prevent lost business.

ACTIVE SOLICITATION

TARP's research shows that actively soliciting customer complaints, comments, and inquiries improves the chances of repeat business even if the complaint, comment, or inquiry is not handled to the customer's satisfaction (or not handled at all). Of course, satisfactorily resolving the complaint or inquiry generates even more loyalty.

This is why traditional productivity measures, such as number of complaints handled this month versus last month or percentage of complaints to transactions, do not tell the story of profitable customer satisfaction. Traditional discussions have asked for guidelines such as

- "Is 2.5 percent of transactions too high for customer complaints?"
- "Should we aim for 1 percent or less to be competitive?"
- "Are 10.11 complaints per 100,000 customers acceptable?"

These measures have been reported in the press, as in "In U.S., Travelers Decry Flight Delays, Overbookings, Poor Service" in the *International Herald Tribune* (June 15, 1987): "In April and May, Continental led the major U.S. airlines in the number of consumer complaints filed and in the number of complaints per 100,000 passengers. Last month, Continental, which is part of Texas Air Corp., registered 21.39 complaints for every 100,000 passengers."

Appropriate questions are the following:

- "Did all the customers with a complaint or inquiry get the opportunity to voice that complaint or inquiry to the company?"

- "How much negative word-of-mouth advertising have we pre-vented?"

- "How many of these customers are purchasing the product or service again?"

Handling complaints and inquiries does cost money. But the most serious problems, or those costing the most to resolve, are the complaints that get voiced. Active solicitation brings out less severe inquiries and problems. Having 50 percent of transactions result in complaints or inquiries would be expensive and probably unprof-itable. However, complaints and inquiries provide the opportunity to educate customers, to cement brand loyalty, to turn negative word-of-mouth advertising into positive word-of-mouth advertis-ing, in fact, to make a profit from perceived service failures.

Companies should make it easier, not harder, for customers to express their opinions and need to approach this activity as a po-tential profit-maker.

POWER AND AUTHORITY

In many companies, the employees handling customer complaints and inquiries are buried deep in the organization at the lowest pay scales and without training. Letters addressed to the managing director may be capably handled by a secretary, but the director never sees them and does not know how many are received. In companies where many complaints deal with billing or price, the employees handling complaints and inquiries are part of the con-troller's area.

Companies vary in the amount and level of attention they give to lost accounts. The people handling customer complaints and in-quiries are accountable for repeat business, specifically for revenue and profit, and they need the power, authority, and level of report within the organization commensurate with this accountability. The complaint and inquiry function should be treated as a profit center, complete with a business plan and budget, repeat business targets, complainant satisfaction tracking, and productivity measures. The function's reports should be read and treated as the priority actions and marketplace feedback that they represent.

STAFFING

Customers with complaints and inquiries expect timely, clear, understandable, and responsive resolution of problems. In return they purchase the product or service again. It is difficult to provide these services without the right employees, properly trained.

In one company, the audit department suggested that complaint and inquiry employees each keep a log for the purpose of monitoring the backlog of complaints. But customers expect a timely response, and a record of a backlog will become a list of customers for the competition. The solution to a backlog must surely be bringing in a team to clear it and then establishing guidelines for responses in line with customers' expectations. If a complaint and inquiry handling unit builds a backlog over a period of time, the permanent staffing levels should be reviewed.

FORM LETTERS

Customers expect an answer to a complaint or inquiry to be responsive to their needs. Form letters—and their verbal counterparts from a toll-free telephone center—help a company save costs and ensure consistency of approach. But the customer's request must be carefully read or heard in order to obtain the true nature and depth of the request. While a request for assistance may seem to require the same resolution or remedy as the last one, the customer's reason for asking may be different and require a different response or a response said in a different way.

The extensive use of form letters to keep answering the same complaint or inquiry might signal a problem that needs preventive analysis and resolution.

CORPORATE POLITICS

The following example shows the damage that can be caused when corporate politics get out of control. A company with retail outlets in over one hundred countries around the world offers customers the convenience of a credit card. Customers can use the card at any location and receive a bill in local currency from the company's head office in their country of residence. A French customer, for example, can make purchases in Hong Kong, New York, Tokyo, and London and receive a bill from the Paris office in French francs.

Customers with a complaint or inquiry are asked to take it up with the local head office in the country where they live. Thus, if French customers have difficulty or a question about their purchases in Tokyo or London, they can speak or write in French to somebody in Paris.

The controller introduces an accounting policy to streamline internal billings. Complaints and inquiries whose remedies fall below a certain limit must be absorbed by the country handling the complaint or inquiry, even if it occurred in another country. These procedures cause the following problems:

1. Customers are pleased to receive a single bill in local currency and to be able to communicate in their own language with someone who can understand their problem or question. However, they soon begin to hear things like, "Oh, Hong Kong again. . . ."

2. Countries with many residents who travel extensively outside the country start to suffer from absorbing the cost of complaints even when their own standards of service delivery are high.

3. Countries having few residents who travel outside the country have many foreign visitors who purchase items in their country. These countries start to make a profit on the new accounting policy.

4. In the countries benefiting from having many visitors from abroad, it becomes easy and profitable to advise customers to

take their complaints or inquiries home and discuss them in their own languages.

5. The result is a vicious circle that involves customers, causing them to escalate complaints and inquiries (which makes the problems more expensive to resolve), spread negative word-of-mouth advertising, switch to competitors, and stop making purchases of any kind from the company, including offices in their countries of residence.

6. The new policy actually rewards poor service delivery, since the country that caused the complaint often is not informed of its failure. Preventive analysis is never done to correct the problems or prevent the problems' recurring in other countries.

Corporate politics are common in companies, corporations, and organizations. But they must be kept internal so that customer satisfaction and repeat business are not affected.

Situations like this may be resolved by implementing customer satisfaction and complainant satisfaction tracking systems, to prove with numbers and facts that customer satisfaction means profit, that making every effort to resolve each perceived service failure creates revenue and profit.

WHEN CUSTOMERS ARE WRONG

Review of customer complaint and inquiry letters and calls usually reveals that in many cases (TARP's research in several companies indicates about one-third), customers are wrong. Most experienced complaint and inquiry handling personnel go out of their way to satisfy the customer the first time, using their response to educate the customer. A helpful tool is a computer system that allows automated recording of this information in case the customer makes contact again with the same problem.

Customers who are wrong and are demanding a sum of money as a remedy can be refused, but the refusal must be timely and accompanied by a clear and understandable explanation. Some judgment must be made of the customer's ability to influence revenues and profits, for example, as a chief executive of a large account, as a member of a vulnerable customer group such as the elderly, or as a person in a position to generate negative publicity. Robert Short, assistant controller for Avis in the United Kingdom with responsibility for the complaint and inquiry handling units, says that his conscience gets the better of him in most of these cases, and he is inclined to give the customer the benefit of the doubt in keeping with the "We try harder." spirit, satisfying the customer even though the complaint may have been a result of the customer being wrong.

Occasionally, circumstances may make a problem situation disproportionately serious to the customer, and a complaint and inquiry handling unit or retail sales outlet may have to face or talk to a very angry person. Patience and skill are required to allow the customer to calm down before an apology is offered and a remedy agreed upon.

HANDSPRINGS CHECKLIST

TARP uses a framework of nineteen functions to evaluate complaint and inquiry handling units and to revise their working methods. At Avis in Europe, these nineteen functions have been adapted into a checklist for ensuring that Avis "does handsprings" to resolve each perceived service failure.

Effective Complaint Management for the Customer

1. Getting Complaints/Inquiries to the Right Place and Prioritizing Them for Action

   - How long does it take for complaints received by the mail room to reach the customer service department?

   - What happens to complaints addressed to senior executives by name or title or to other departments?

- Are all complaint receivers aware of where to send the complaints and the importance of immediate forwarding?

- To whom does the central switchboard operator direct customers who call with a problem or inquiry?

- If the call is misdirected, do other employees know where to direct the call or how to handle the call?

- What do departments other than the customer service department do with incoming complaint and inquiry calls?

- Is a separate direct line (or toll-free line) needed?

- Do customer service department employees have written guidelines on how to spot and what to do with serious complaints that deserve priority?

- Do all employees who receive a written or telephone complaint know what the company prioritization of complaints is and what action to take?

2. Logging the Complaints/Inquiries

- Is there an access identifier or unique code, customer name, or any other piece of information that enables the complaint to be easily retrieved for future action?

- Does the log contain action responsibility or a record of who is handling the complaint, a target date for response, and action to be taken?

- Is progress information logged, including the date the complaint was received and the date it was answered?

- Is the complaint categorized in an actionable way to enable preventative analysis?

- If complaints received by telephone are resolved immediately, is any notation made of the root cause and complaint category?

- Are all complaints logged to the same degree?

3. Categorizing the Complaints/Inquiries

- Does the categorization record the problems being complained about as perceived by the customer?

- Does the categorization identify the specific service or product being complained about?

- Does the categorization record who was responsible for the problem?

- Does the categorization identify the root cause of the problem, i.e., company policy, procedure, system, employee error, wrong customer expectation?

- Does the categorization track escalation and reasons for the escalation?

- How large is the "miscellaneous" category (if more than 5 percent, additional categories are needed)?

- Are the categories specific enough for preventive action to be taken?

4. Investigating the Complaints/Inquiries

- Do complaint-handling employees know where to go to get the information necessary to investigate the complaint?

- How long does it take to investigate complaints?

- How often does an employee have to request additional information beyond the original request and on what types of complaints is this done?

- How specific are the requests for information to investigate complaints?

5. Answering the Complaints/Inquiries

- Do answers immediately meet customer expectations or explain why the customer's expectations cannot be met?

- Do answers provide reassurance if further investigation is required to resolve the complaint or inquiry?

- Are answers comprehensive, answering all of the customer's complaint points or inquiries?

- Are answers clear and understandable to the customer?

- Are answers accurate?

- Are answers timely?

- Do the answers consider long-term market benefits of repeat business?

6. Producing the Responses

   - Are responses clear and free of technical jargon?

   - Are responses appropriately worded?

   - Are responses accurate, i.e., correct terms used by telephone, correct terms used in written correspondence?

   - Are responses accurate, i.e., stated in the right way by telephone, written and typed accurately in correspondence?

   - Are responses produced on a timely basis?

7. Distributing the Responses

   - Are responses distributed on a timely basis?

   - Do responses always reach customers, which means having correct addresses?

   - Do information copies go to other persons and departments in the company that can take action on problem areas?

8. Storing and Retrieving Data

   - Are details of complaints and inquiries and how they were resolved complete?

   - Can these details be accessed easily?

Effective Complaint Management for the Company

9. Managing Timely Responses

   - Are all complaints and inquiries answered within the time frame expected by customers?

   - Is there an accurate way of measuring and reporting response time?

10. Following Up on Referrals

- Are complaints and inquiries referred to other offices for handling sampled regularly to ensure that they are being actioned according to the same standards?

- Is corrective action initiated when referral offices fail to effectively manage referred complaints and inquiries?

11. Preparing Monthly Reports

- Are monthly reports prepared and submitted on time and with complete details each month?

- Are monthly reports distributed to the appropriate managers in the organization?

- Do monthly reports include productivity statistics such as number of complaints resolved in the specified categories, cost of operating the complaint and inquiry handling unit, cost of remedies, and response times?

- Do monthly reports include the status of preventive recommendations?

- Do monthly reports include meaningful business statistics such as the satisfaction levels and return on investment of the complaint and inquiry handling unit?

12. Identifying and Analyzing Problems

- Does the complaint and inquiry handling unit identify the root causes of problems and analyze what can be done to prevent the problems from recurring?

- Does the complaint and inquiry handling unit quantify the market damage for key problems and place them in priority order?

13. Recommending Preventive Measures

- Does the complaint and inquiry handling unit produce a priority listing of key problems for correction and prevention in priority order according to market damage?

- Are these recommendations presented to the appropriate managers in the organization who can correct the problem or prevent it from recurring?

- Does the complaint and inquiry handling unit follow up on the preventive measures taken to eliminate problems?

14. Evaluating the Function

- Does the complaint and inquiry handling unit meet the standards for timely responses?

- Do they submit monthly reports on time with complete data and information?

- Do they produce preventive recommendations that are acted upon?

- Do they show increasing levels of customer satisfaction and repurchase intention?

- Do they show an increasing return on investment?

15. Planning for Return on Investment

- Does the complaint and inquiry handling unit produce a business plan and profit plan according to the company's timetable for business planning?

- Does the plan include response timeliness goals?

- Does the plan include improvements to effective complaint management for the customer?

- Does the plan include staffing levels, costs, and volume projections?

- Does the plan include preventive recommendation goals and projected resulting market benefit?

- Does the plan include the planned return on investment?

- Does the plan include staff selection, training, incentives, and development goals?

16. Tracking Customer Satisfaction

    - Does the complaint and inquiry handling unit operate a satisfaction tracking system to track satisfaction levels and repurchase intention?

    - Do they use this to evaluate their performance and calculate return on investment?

17. Managing Accountability

    - Is the complaint and inquiry handling unit accountable for turning dissatisfied customers into satisfied customers, for generating positive word-of-mouth advertising, and for getting customers to purchase the product or service again to produce return on investment?

    - Is the complaint and inquiry handling unit accountable for identifying root causes of complaints and inquiries and making preventive recommendations?

    - Are these accountabilities written and endorsed by senior management?

18. Selecting, Training, and Developing Staff

    - Are there appropriate standards for recruiting and selecting staff?

    - Are new staff given training before they take up their new jobs?

    - Are existing staff given training in new procedures, policies, and computer systems?

    - Are there incentives or reward and recognition programs to encourage outstanding service performance?

    - Are there development opportunities for complaint and inquiry handling staff?

19. Getting Customers to Inquire and Complain

    - Do customers know how and where to inquire or complain?

    - Is it easy for customers to make an inquiry or complaint?

GUIDELINES FOR CHIEF EXECUTIVES

Chief executives must be vitally concerned with effective complaint management as a revenue and profit-producer for the company. TARP uses the formula that doing the job right the first time plus effective complaint management equals maximum customer satisfaction and brand loyalty. Just as they review revenue and profit figures for what is in most cases over 80 percent of the business (the job being done right the first time), so must executives look at the revenue and profit figures generated from effective complaint management.

Chief executives should routinely consider:

1. Do I know how many customers are dissatisfied with the service my company provides?

2. Do I know how many of these dissatisfied customers are encouraged to communicate their complaint or inquiry to my company?

3. What percentage of repeat business do my company's complaint and inquiry handling personnel generate from the complaints and inquiries they handle?

4. Do I know how much return on investment my complaint and inquiry handling function generates?

5. Do I know how many complaints and inquiries are addressed personally to me?

6. If I meet a customer with a complaint or inquiry, do I know how to handle it and do I handle it?

GUIDELINES FOR FRONT-LINE SERVICE DELIVERY PERSONNEL

Front-line service delivery personnel are the first to hear a customer's complaint or inquiry. Their handling of customers is the first opportunity to create loyalty to the company.

When facing angry, irate, or even abusive customers front-line employees should remember that customers are angry about the service and not at them personally. As anger mounts, the ability to reason deteriorates. These customers must be listened to calmly until the anger abates. Employees may then apologize and agree upon corrective action.

Front-line service delivery personnel hold the key to repeat business from dissatisfied customers. They must ask themselves the following:

1. Do I serve each and every customer in a manner that will make this customer want to purchase my company's products and services again?

2. When a customer has a question, do I take the time to offer a clear and responsive explanation?

3. When many customers have the same question or problem, do I recommend improvements through the channels available to me?

4. Do I use all available tools and authority to resolve customers' questions and problems the moment they occur?

5. When a customer has a problem, do I view this as an opportunity to turn this customer into a loyal customer of my company?

6. When I have to deal with an angry customer, do I first listen calmly to allow the customer's anger to ease before proceeding with an apology and agreement on a course of action?

7. Do I actively ask customers if they are satisfied with the service and take interest in and, if necessary, action on what they say?

8. Do I know how to fix or remedy the problems my customers have so that they are satisfied? Have I attended the appropriate training programs and learned all that I can about how to solve customers' problems?

9. Do I actively look for sources of potential problems (e.g., a building line of waiting customers) and try to the best of my

ability to say or do something to prevent the problem or ease the situation?

GUIDELINES FOR BACK-OFFICE SERVICE SUPPORT PERSONNEL

Back-office service support personnel have little opportunity to handle customer inquiries and problems directly. However, their job duties support the service being given to customers, including the ability of front-line service delivery personnel to answer questions and solve problems.

Back-office service support personnel should consider the following:

1. Do I carry out my job duties in a manner that will cause each and every customer to want to purchase my company's products and services again?

2. Do I use all available tools and authority and all of my skills and knowledge to help front-line service delivery personnel answer a question or solve a problem whenever they ask me for help?

3. Do I actively look for sources of potential problems in my own work area and contribute ideas for improvement through the channels available to me?

GUIDELINES FOR MIDDLE MANAGEMENT

Middle managers, like chief executives, should focus their attention not just on the 80 percent or more of the business that is generating revenue and profit by doing the job right the first time, but also on effective complaint management, which also generates revenue and profit. Middle managers inevitably are drawn into customer inquiries and complaints when:

- they're working late in a headquarters office and pick up a phone call from a customer,

- they come in early and pick up a phone call from a front-line service delivery employee asking for help in dealing with a dissatisfied customer,

- a switchboard or another department passes them a call from a customer,

- they're on a business trip and sit next to one of their company's customers on the airplane,

- they're at a cocktail party and chat with another guest who is one of their company's customers,

- they speak at or attend an external conference or seminar and meet one of their company's customers, or

- they are in countless other business and social settings with other people.

Middle management is where policy is often formulated, policy that has impact on effective complaint management. And it is in middle management that company politics are often most intense. Middle managers should consider the following:

1. When I am drawn into a customer inquiry or problem, do I know how to handle it and do I handle it so that the customer will want to use my company's products and services again?
2. In the political arena, do I give the customer's needs top priority?
3. Do I actively encourage my company's employees to submit ideas for improvements to effective complaint management and do I move these ideas forward?
4. Do I understand the revenue, profit, and return on investment that are possible from effective complaint management?

11

Measure, Evaluate, and Pay Attention to Actual Service Delivery

In 1981, a national service company with over three thousand U.S. locations focused its attention on declining revenues, profits, and market share. Extreme cost reduction measures were taken: head office staffing levels were cut, field procedures were rationalized, advertising budgets were slashed, and the sales force received stiff targets. The chief executive and his inner circle had visited locations infrequently and when on site failed to notice the service being given and the condition of the offices and staff. On the sides of their desks, unread, were the detailed reports of the quality assurance team that continued to rigorously inspect and report a steady decline in service. Also on the sides of their desks, unread, were detailed reports from the customer service department, with ever-growing lists of urgent preventive recommendations for problems that had never before existed and detailed statistics that accurately logged and reported a steady increase in customer complaints. Yet these reports never entered into the discussions of how to halt the decline in revenues, market share, and profit.

PAYING ATTENTION TO ACTUAL SERVICE DELIVERY

Can this same situation happen today? Yes, even in the same company, because service delivery and customer satisfaction must be looked after with diligence, zeal, even obsession.

Thomas J. Peters and Robert H. Waterman, Jr., in *In Search of Excellence* (1982), devote a chapter to what they call "staying close to the customer." "A simple summary of what our research uncovered on the customer attribute is this: the excellent companies really are close to their customers. That's it. Other companies talk about it; the excellent companies do it."

In fact, talking about customer service, quality of service, superior service, and service excellence is fashionable and is a discussion to which almost everyone can contribute. Says Philip Crosby in *Quality Is Free* (1979), "quality has much in common with sex. Everyone is for it. (Under certain conditions, of course.) Everyone feels they understand it. (Even though they wouldn't want to explain it.) Everyone thinks execution is only a matter of following natural inclinations. (After all, we do get along somehow.) And, of course, most people feel that all problems in these areas are caused by other people. (If only they would take the time to do things right.)" It is not enough to talk about it, not enough to discuss it intelligently, not enough to speak about it passionately. Our talks and discussions must get turned into actions, our passions into committed initiatives.

To turn talk into action, we must first pay attention to actual service delivery—with the exact same diligence, passion, and obsession with which we study profit performance. Paying attention to actual service delivery means measuring service delivery and analyzing the results. The measurement needs to be both from external and internal sources to get a realistic and balanced picture. But the most sophisticated measurement in the world is only as good as the use we make of it—the decisions and actions we take after reviewing and analyzing it.

QUALITY ASSURANCE TEAMS

As a method of internal measurement, many companies employ quality assurance teams that inspect service delivery locations against a set of standards, producing reports and statistics that show how each location measures up to the standards. This method is often used in organizations with dispersed service delivery points.

The success of a quality assurance team is built upon the standards against which performance will be evaluated. The standards must be set in line with customers' expectations. An example is having to deliver service in a facility under construction or renovation or in one that has been damaged by violent weather. Service delivery and service support personnel at such a location will claim that lowered scores or poor reports are justified and that they have been working twice as hard as usual to overcome a situation they did not cause. But despite the impact on morale, customer expectations must be met or exceeded, although market research may indicate that customers' expectations are slightly lower in such a situation.

Measurement against standards must be fair and as objective as possible. Most companies provide initial training for quality assurance team members to ensure fair and consistent measurement and reporting. Training is important in companies that use the quality assurance team positions in job rotation schemes or as a development ground for career progression.

Despite the job rotation employees often immediately recognize team members. This prompts management to worry that a location will get a good score or report only by "cleaning up their act" to impress the quality assurance team. But a quality assurance team is measuring both the service being delivered and the location's service delivery capability. Immediate sighting of a quality assurance team will not replace a burned out sign, clean a dirty office, or make a backlog of administrative paperwork disappear. And employees deliberately showing off superior personal service skills and attitudes at least demonstrate that they have them and know how to use them. Performance deterioration will show up in other measurement methods.

The reports and statistics produced by a quality assurance team should be easily and quickly produced by the team as well as easily and quickly read and understood by management. Charts and graphs that show increases or decreases as well as one-page ratings that show improvements or deteriorations in service levels are both useful for clear reports.

Because a quality assurance team may be among the few in an organization who visit several service delivery locations making objective and measured comparisons, they can suggest improvements and encourage sharing of ideas. Their constructive suggestions should be used fully.

CUSTOMER SERVICE REPORTS

Reports and statistics prepared regularly by the customer service department or the company's complaint and inquiry handling units are often used to measure service delivery. Because these reports are prepared in-house, they are considered internal measurement, but, of course, they represent a portion of customer opinion. TARP's research offers new ways of interpreting the data.

The most important factor in customer complaints and inquiries is not how many occur but rather how many do not, and whether those who did complain or inquire will purchase the product or service again as a result of the way the complaint or inquiry was handled. One cannot assume that service delivery is increasing because the number of complaints and inquiries has decreased.

The most important parts of the customer service department's reports are the repurchase intention, the return on investment, and the preventive recommendations for taking action to prevent the problem from recurring. Said another way, the number of complaints handled by a customer service department does not measure the level of service being given by a company, but only how many people complained.

The customer service department or the complaint and inquiry handling units are themselves service delivery points. The number of complaints and inquiries they handle is their volume or productivity in the same way as the number of transactions or customers processed by a service delivery point is their volume or productivity. The measurement for the customer service department or the complaint and inquiry handling units is the service they give that causes customers to spread positive word-of-mouth advertising and to purchase the product or service again.

AUDITS

While the audit department is often thought of as focusing on internal controls, company policies, and procedures, many companies have begun to use it to audit service standards and service delivery as well. The audit department in most companies possesses an important qualification for this duty, namely clout. Their reports and recommendations are read, actioned, and replied to.

The audit department's measurement methods and techniques may be similar to those of quality assurance teams. In fact, some companies simply expand the audit staff to accommodate this function without investing in a separate quality assurance team.

SELF-AUDITS

Whether a company uses a quality assurance team, the audit department, or both to provide internal measurement of service delivery, front-line service delivery supervisors and managers must know the standards by which they are evaluated and the importance of these standards to customers.

One successful and simple measurement to use is self-audits or self-audit checklists. These should contain the same standards as those used by the quality assurance team and/or the audit department. They allow supervisors and managers to check their own service delivery locations or areas of responsibility against the standards.

Some companies require supervisors and managers to routinely conduct self-audits and report the results, using this as a means of reducing the frequency of visits or supplementing visits by the quality assurance team and/or the audit department. This embeds quality checking in the jobs of front-line service delivery supervisors and managers, and holds them accountable for their own service delivery. To counteract supervisors' and managers' subjectivity or bias, a program goal should be for supervisors' and managers' self-audits to agree with those of the quality assurance team and/or audit department.

Self-audits focus attention on service delivery in all areas of the organization and involve many employees in measuring and attending to it.

QUALITY CIRCLES AND FOCUS GROUPS

Quality circles and focus groups are often the catalysts for developing a program of self-audits. As they identify and resolve quality problems or failures in meeting customers' expectations, they represent the leading edge of internal measurement and evaluation.

Management may see one disadvantage of their measurement and evaluation as a lack of objective comparison data between locations, but this is actually their strength. Because they usually work at only one location or service delivery point, they tend to measure and evaluate in terms of their own views and the expectations of their own customers. Much can be achieved with localized measurement and evaluation of service delivery, as long as locally adopted policies and procedures do not work at cross-purposes with company goals and service strategy.

EMPLOYEE SURVEYS

The employees who speak to, write to, and face customers daily, as well as those in service support positions, are valuable assets to a company in measuring, evaluating, and paying attention to actual service delivery. These employees are often the first to know and recognize when a new service offering is not well-received by customers or well-executed by the company.

Employee surveys are an organized method for getting employee input as an internal measurement of actual service delivery. However, most companies using written questionnaires to survey employees do so too infrequently to continuously measure actual service delivery. The evaluation and verification process in which employee views tend to support opinions obtained from customers is important. Surveys also have value in identifying those areas where employees feel they are blocked from delivering superior service to customers by company policies, awkward procedures, accounting controls, and system restrictions.

Informal employee surveys may be done more frequently by telephone or personal contact. However, in some organizations, getting employees to openly express their opinions has required hiring external consultants to do survey work, with only summarized results being supplied to the company's management.

VISIBLE MANAGEMENT

Bridging the gap between internal and external measurements is the procedure known as visible management, which periodically schedules senior executives and middle managers to work in front-line service delivery positions where they have direct contact with customers and employees.

When a visible management assignment is done properly, the senior executive or middle manager must speak to customers and to employees and gain an impression of the actual service being delivered. Visible management assignments also help verify data obtained from other measurement sources. If the audit department, for example, has reported specific problems in one location, a visible management assignment in that same location can help clarify the needed remedial actions.

Visible management also allows employees to express their opinions and ideas to senior and middle managers in the familiarity of their own environment where they can often demonstrate points and ideas that lose impact when forwarded through channels.

CUSTOMER AUDITS

External measurement of actual service delivery is essential to balance internal measurement. A simple method to measure customer reaction is to ask selected customers to audit actual service delivery. This method may be used as a selling tool.

If, for example, a hotel chain signs an agreement to accommodate a company's business travelers, the hotel may ask that 1 or 2 percent of the travelers complete an audit checklist of the service in return for a free night or a free meal. This provides an opportunity for the hotel to educate some customers about service standards as well as deliver the message that their opinion is valued. The client company feels that it is contributing to improvements in actual service delivery for the benefit of its own employees or travelers. The same technique may be used with traveling managers and executives of one's own company if they, too, must use the service as a customer. A key benefit of customer audits is obtaining ideas and opinions for service improvement from frequent purchasers of the services.

CUSTOMER SATISFACTION TRACKING SYSTEMS

The best judges of whether actual service delivery is meeting or exceeding customer expectations are, of course, customers. Measuring customer opinion is crucial to the success of any company that sells products and services for profit.

Annual or semiannual or even one-time surveys may be used to get an in-depth reading of customer satisfaction. Generally, a representative sample of customers is selected and interviewed by telephone or in person or asked to complete a questionnaire. Customer satisfaction surveys should ask how satisfied customers are with service delivery, what problems were experienced, whether assistance to answer a question or solve a problem was sought and where the customer sought advice, how many people the customer told about the experience (good or bad), and whether the customer intends to purchase the product or service again. Surveys may be used in a variety of ways: to measure satisfaction with specific programs or service offerings, to measure satisfaction in specific geographic areas, or to measure interest in other product and service offerings of the company. According to TARP, surveys generally justify their cost or produce a positive return on investment, if only because customers' intention to repurchase increases only by their being asked for an opinion. Also, surveys generally uncover at least one major problem, such as an entire account planning to switch brands, and this information enables the company to avert the loss of business. Individual consumers or customers and accounts may be surveyed.

Many companies run customer satisfaction tracking systems on a continuous basis. These systems may consist of comment or rating cards readily available at service delivery points, postcard-style questionnaires mailed to recent customers as direct mail or with bills, routine telephone research, or service delivery personnel asking for comments and ratings and recording them in front of customers. The tracking systems should ask if customers were satisfied with the service and whether they intend to purchase the product or service again. Satisfaction with individual products and services, with specific geographic locations, or with specific employees or teams of employees can be measured in this way. Results should be tabulated quickly and distributed to the employees responsible for the service delivery being measured.

Customer satisfaction must be measured for each area of customer contact that affects the customer's decision to buy. In the travel industry, this contact area includes centralized reservation centers and customers' ability to reach them and obtain a reservation. In most companies, this involves the complaint and inquiry handling units, which contribute profit by generating repeat business. Often overlooked areas are the central switchboard of a headquarters office that receives calls from customers, and the billing process and whether it results in accurate and understandable billings.

The data obtained from customer satisfaction surveys and tracking systems may be used in a variety of ways: to correct specific performance deficiencies, to identify problems for correction, to supply data to a variety of economic models on the profit impact of causes of dissatisfaction and the revenue opportunities of sources of satisfaction.

Satisfaction measurement, of course, must get to the decision-maker in the buying process. If a company's customers are other companies, then these companies' satisfaction must be measured.

Whatever methods are used to obtain the data, customer satisfaction results must reach all of the concerned areas of the organization, and they must be evaluated and heeded to balance customer satisfaction and company profits. When customer expectations are met or exceeded they have a tendency to increase, and service-obsessed companies never see the end of programs and actions to improve service. In short, the marketplace never stands still.

MARKET RESEARCH

Market research is generally undertaken to obtain and verify customer needs to support the development of new products or service offerings. However, market research can also measure and evaluate actual service delivery, either coincidentally or intentionally.

Market research is particularly important where market share growth or market growth is desired (or where one or both are declining). Customer satisfaction tracking systems measure the satisfaction of those customers who have recently purchased or are currently purchasing products and services. But these systems cannot predict the possible satisfaction of new customers or discover the reasons why past customers have stopped purchasing products and services. For these purposes, market research is needed.

A variation or supplement to market research "mystery shopping," or paying people to sample a product or service, was described by David Evans in *Marketing Week* (February 19, 1988) in "Setting Standards in Customer Care." He said, "One of the sharpest tools to research your customer image is the method called 'mystery shopping.' This involves exposing your naked commercial body to some objective views of people who are not professional market researchers—they are paid yet objective panellists who literally shop your commercial proposition."

Market research and mystery shopping can provide valuable data, but the data must be evaluated and used to improve service delivery.

FINANCIAL IMPACT

In corporate boardrooms the atmosphere is alive with numbers and financial data—profit or loss figures, revenue growth or decline, market share increase or decrease—on walls, on screens, in executive folders. If customer satisfaction is to be a topic in these boardrooms, it must be expressed in numbers and financial impact.

All measurements must build a financial picture of customer satisfaction:

- that dissatisfied customers tell others, some of whom then don't buy the product or service, resulting in lost revenues,

- that dissatisfied customers sometimes do not communicate their dissatisfaction but switch brands, resulting in lost revenues,

- that customers who have complained or inquired have been responded to so well that many of them are telling others, some of whom will buy the product or service and create incremental revenues, and that many of them are purchasing the product or service again, resulting in revenues gained without marketing or advertising expenditure,

- that satisfied customers tell others, some of whom will buy the product or service and create revenues gained without marketing or advertising expenditure,

- that eliminating the root cause of a source of customer dissatisfaction will result in a revenue opportunity,

- that frowns took X percent off the bottom line, or

- that smiles put Y percent on the bottom line.

CONTINUOUS COMMITMENT

Financial data are often used to compare companies in the same or different industries. Service performance, which is more subjective than that supported by numeric data, is certainly used by consumers to compare brands. But what should be a company's service goal: to be better than industry competitors, to be better than all service companies, to aim for 100 percent customer satisfaction? These are some of the tangled trade-offs or conflicting comparisons that face today's service companies. Should they be committed to superior service, service-oriented, or be service-obsessed?

There are no magic formulas, no one recipe for success. But several things are clear. A company must measure, evaluate, and pay attention to actual service delivery. There must be continuous, permanent commitment to this activity.

GUIDELINES FOR CHIEF EXECUTIVES

A KLM print ad in 1986 stated, "98 percent of our passengers vote KLM first-rate. So there is still room for improvement." Should a chief executive be satisfied with this figure?

Chief executives play a key role in attending to actual service delivery and seeing that measurement and evaluation of service delivery are carried out. The questions to ask are simple: Do I know what service is actually being delivered by my company and do I know this at all times?

GUIDELINES FOR FRONT-LINE SERVICE DELIVERY PERSONNEL

Employees in front-line service delivery positions know when customers are satisfied or unhappy, if they are paying attention.

At the Vidal Sassoon salon near Covent Garden in London, manager John Ratcliffe and his staff step delicately back into the narrow walkway of the tiny hairdressing salon in the important ritual near the end of each customer's visit. They hold mirrors at just the right angles to let customers see each view of their new hair style. The mirror doesn't move to the next angle until stylist's and customer's eyes meet in the wall mirror and customer satisfaction is measured.

Whether one's job includes direct measurement of customer satisfaction, as at Vidal Sassoon, front-line employees must pay attention to service delivery and customers' reactions and consider the following:

1. Do I participate fully in any self-audits that I am asked to do?

2. Do I participate fully in quality circles, focus groups, and employee surveys?

3. Do I support my company's customer satisfaction tracking systems by displaying comment or rating cards and by encouraging customers to complete questionnaires?

4. When a customer hesitates or appears to have a question or a problem, do I readily offer assistance?

5. Do I offer suggestions for service improvement through the channels open to me?

6. Do I actively look for signs of customer satisfaction (e.g., a smile or a "thank you" from the customer) and actively ask customers if they're satisfied with the service provided?

GUIDELINES FOR BACK-OFFICE SERVICE SUPPORT PERSONNEL

Back-office service support employees have little opportunity to see and know when customers are satisfied with actual service delivery. However, their jobs support front-line service delivery and sometimes deal directly with measurement and evaluation. Because actual service delivery and the level of service the company gives to customers is related to the company's profit and success, service support can never escape its accountability, along with the rest of the company's employees, for paying attention to actual service delivery.

GUIDELINES FOR MIDDLE MANAGEMENT

Middle managers control front-line service delivery teams, back-office service support teams, and teams that carry out support functions directly affecting service delivery. Middle managers play a vital role in measuring, evaluating, and paying attention to actual service delivery. For some, daily jobs will involve measurement and evaluation of the company's service delivery. For managers in excellent service companies, incentive plans will be linked to the service delivered by their teams.

Middle managers should consider the following:

1. Do my team and I pay attention to actual service delivery and know at all times what the company's service levels are?

2. Do my team and I participate fully in any self-audits that are used?

3. Do my team and I support our company's customer satisfaction tracking systems and encourage customers to respond to them?

4. Do I pass along ideas for service improvement that I receive from my team and other colleagues?

5. Do I regularly schedule myself for visible management assignments and make the most of these for evaluating and paying attention to actual service delivery?

6. Do I read and study quality assurance reports, audit reports, and customer service reports about my areas of responsibility and take immediate action to solve problems and improve service?

7. Am I able to discuss customer satisfaction and actual service delivery in numeric terms with financial impact?

12

How to Move a Company to Service Excellence (and Keep It There)

The most difficult part of moving a company to service excellence is not generating the ideas but rather executing the ideas—and continuing to execute the ideas that allow a company to continue in the dynamic state of service excellence. Whether one is the chief executive, an external consultant, or an employee anywhere in the organization, a checklist to identify where actions are needed is a good place to begin.

THE SERVICE EXCELLENCE CHECKLIST

I. Name of Company or Organization _____
   Dates of Assessment _____

II. Level of Commitment   NO   YES

   1. Is there a senior executive who appears
      committed to service excellence?   ☐   ☐

	NO	YES
2. Is there a senior executive who appears to be a skeptic about service excellence?	☐	☐
3. Does the company have an ample supply of "service classics" (books on service such as *In Search of Excellence, Service America, Quality Is Free*) and current newspaper and magazine articles to give to the committed and the skeptical senior executives to read?	☐	☐
4. Can we or the service-committed senior executive reach the chief executive and obtain his or her commitment?	☐	☐
5. Can we or the service-committed senior executive get a written statement of commitment from the chief executive?	☐	☐
6. Can an initial funding commitment in the range of 4 percent of the marketing budget or .13 percent of revenues be obtained?	☐	☐
7. Can approval be obtained to form an interdisciplinary group of the company's best people, including one skeptic, to look at service excellence?	☐	☐
8. Is there a service strategy or can one be written from initial research and can agreement on it be obtained?	☐	☐
9. Do the senior executives see the crisis or can it be demonstrated effectively?	☐	☐
10. Can time commitments and priorities for the company's other initiatives be overcome so that service excellence has the proper time commitment and priority?	☐	☐
11. Does the company need to increase profits (market, market share, or revenues)?	☐	☐

A full set of "yesses" must be checked in order to proceed, particularly for items 5 and 6, which are known as passing the pen and passing the hat.

	No Immediate Attention Needed	Attention May Be Needed	Urgent Attention Needed
III. The Right People	3	2	1
1. Do job descriptions exist for all employees (either as formal written documents or as clearly defined ideas in the minds of employees) and does each job description specify how the job relates to delivering customer satisfaction?	☐	☐	☐
2. Do person specifications or a defined list of skills exist for each job in the company or organization?	☐	☐	☐
3. Are the service skills and attitudes needed for customer contact positions properly defined?	☐	☐	☐
4. Do all recruitment messages deliver a strong message to prospective applicants about the company's commitment to service excellence?	☐	☐	☐
5. Are all prospective applicants interviewed carefully and "what if" situations posed in interviews?	☐	☐	☐
6. Is reference checking done before all offers of employment?	☐	☐	☐
7. Are interviewing and reference checking supported by testing and/or psychological evaluation of service skills and attitudes for all customer contact positions?	☐	☐	☐
8. Are employment agencies used effectively?	☐	☐	☐
9. Are salary and benefit offerings competitive within the industry or skill base to attract the right people?	☐	☐	☐

	No Immediate Attention Needed	Attention May Be Needed	Urgent Attention Needed
	3	2	1
10. Are probationary periods used as a positive trial for both employer and employee?	☐	☐	☐
11. Are exit interviews used to maximum benefit?	☐	☐	☐
12. Do employee surveys or other data support the statement that the company is hiring the right people to deliver service?	☐	☐	☐

Items checked "1"—urgent attention needed—form the basis for the Customer Satisfaction Business Plan.

IV. Organizational Structure

1. Is there a service strategy and do all or most of the company's employees know what it is?	☐	☐	☐
2. Are there methods and ways by which front-line service delivery personnel can originate and put forth ideas to increase customer satisfaction?	☐	☐	☐
3. Are there methods and ways by which back-office service support personnel can originate and put forth ideas to increase customer satisfaction?	☐	☐	☐
4. Do ideas originate and get executed, both successfully and unsuccessfully?	☐	☐	☐
5. Do opportunities exist for many people in the organization to "buy in" to ideas?	☐	☐	☐
6. Do opportunities exist for many people in the organization to participate in the execution of ideas?	☐	☐	☐

	No Immediate Attention Needed	Attention May Be Needed	Urgent Attention Needed
	3	2	1
7. Are the successes of ideas measured, either subjectively or objectively, and evaluated?	☐	☐	☐
8. Are there sufficient job rotation opportunities, and are they exercised?	☐	☐	☐
9. Are there sufficient job engineering opportunities, and are they exercised?	☐	☐	☐
10. Are visible management, management by walking about, and other such techniques used to keep management in touch with employees and customers?	☐	☐	☐
11. Are there sufficient opportunities for promotion and advancement within the company, and are they exercised?	☐	☐	☐
12. Are there sufficient opportunities for job enrichment, and are they exercised?	☐	☐	☐
13. Are there sufficient opportunities for, and is attention given to, the development of all employees' conceptual skills?	☐	☐	☐
14. Is there a workable balance among power groups in support of the service strategy?	☐	☐	☐

Items checked as "1"—urgent attention needed—form the basis for the Customer Satisfaction Business Plan.

V. Training and Development

1. Is there a comprehensive overall training plan for all employees in support of the service strategy?	☐	☐	☐
2. Is technical skills training provided to new employees to enable them to do their jobs?	☐	☐	☐

	No Immediate Attention Needed	Attention May Be Needed	Urgent Attention Needed
	3	2	1
3. Is technical skills training provided in support of new methods, new procedures, and new products?	☐	☐	☐
4. Is behavioral skills training provided to new customer contact employees to enable them to do their jobs?	☐	☐	☐
5. Is behavioral skills training provided to newly promoted or about-to-be-promoted employees?	☐	☐	☐
6. Is behavioral skills training provided in support of new service offerings?	☐	☐	☐
7. Are technical and behavioral skills taught in training programs reinforced and encouraged on-the-job?	☐	☐	☐
8. Are there sufficient elements of conceptual skills training?	☐	☐	☐
9. Is there a balance of technical skills, behavioral skills, and conceptual skills training?	☐	☐	☐
10. Do the training techniques used achieve the instructional objectives in the most cost-effective manner?	☐	☐	☐
11. Is on-the-job training given in the most effective manner?	☐	☐	☐
12. Is employee participation in training and development programs encouraged and given the necessary priority?	☐	☐	☐
13. Is optimum use made of external consultants and materials in support of the comprehensive overall training plan?	☐	☐	☐

	No Immediate Attention Needed	Attention May Be Needed	Urgent Attention Needed
	3	2	1

14. Are there sufficient opportunities for personal growth and development? ☐ ☐ ☐

Items checked "1"—urgent attention needed—form the basis for the Customer Satisfaction Business Plan.

VI. Product/Service Perception

1. Are the products and services being delivered of sufficient quality? ☐ ☐ ☐

2. Does the service strategy support perception of superior product/service? ☐ ☐ ☐

3. Do the prices support perception of superior product/service? ☐ ☐ ☐

4. Do the appearance and atmosphere of all product and service delivery points seen or heard by customers support perception of superior product/service? ☐ ☐ ☐

5. Do the attitudes and mannerisms of the front-line service delivery personnel support perception of superior product/service? ☐ ☐ ☐

6. Do the advertising messages support perception of superior product/service? ☐ ☐ ☐

7. Is customer perception of the product/service tested and the results evaluated regularly? ☐ ☐ ☐

8. Is employee perception of the product/service tested and the results evaluated regularly? ☐ ☐ ☐

9. Is customer opinion solicited regularly? ☐ ☐ ☐

	No Immediate Attention Needed	Attention May Be Needed	Urgent Attention Needed
	3	2	1
10. Do public relations activities support perception of superior product/service?	☐	☐	☐

Items checked "1"—urgent attention needed—form the basis for the Customer Satisfaction Business Plan.

VII. Performance

1. Do all employees know the company's service strategy?	☐	☐	☐
2. Are there service standards based on customer expectations?	☐	☐	☐
3. Do service standards exist for both normal operating conditions and for extraordinary conditions?	☐	☐	☐
4. Do the service standards inspire exceptional performance?	☐	☐	☐
5. Do all job descriptions feature customer satisfaction as top priority?	☐	☐	☐
6. Are job descriptions flexible and broad enough to allow exceptional performance and total customer satisfaction?	☐	☐	☐
7. Do targets and objectives feature customer satisfaction as top priority?	☐	☐	☐
8. Do performance appraisals take up the issue of customer satisfaction as top priority?	☐	☐	☐
9. Do promotions take customer satisfaction performance into consideration as top priority?	☐	☐	☐

	No Immediate Attention Needed	Attention May Be Needed	Urgent Attention Needed
	3	2	1

10. Do daily supervision activities gear performance to deliver service as a number one priority? ☐ ☐ ☐

11. Under extraordinary operating conditions, does customer satisfaction remain as top priority? ☐ ☐ ☐

12. Does the company's management style treat employees in the manner that the company would like its customers treated? ☐ ☐ ☐

Items checked "1"—urgent attention needed—form the basis for the Customer Satisfaction Business Plan.

VIII. Opportunity

1. Are staffing levels sufficient to support the company's service strategy? ☐ ☐ ☐

2. Are all staff trained to do their jobs, including part-time and temporary staff? ☐ ☐ ☐

3. Is there sufficient team spirit among all employees? ☐ ☐ ☐

4. Do performance standards inspire exceptional performance? ☐ ☐ ☐

5. Are there performance standards for both routine and nonroutine situations? ☐ ☐ ☐

6. Do policies and procedures support the company's service strategy as well as providing proper controls? ☐ ☐ ☐

7. Is there sufficient opportunity for the development and exercise of conceptual skills as customer expectations rise? ☐ ☐ ☐

	No Immediate Attention Needed	Attention May Be Needed	Urgent Attention Needed
	3	2	1
8. Are employees sufficiently empowered to deliver superior service in all situations?	☐	☐	☐
9. Do feedback systems exist and get used regularly for recognizing compliments?	☐	☐	☐
10. Do incentive schemes support the company's service strategy?	☐	☐	☐
11. Are there sufficient reward and recognition schemes for customer satisfaction?	☐	☐	☐
12. Are service offerings continuously in tune with customer needs?	☐	☐	☐
13. Are customer education materials provided where needed?	☐	☐	☐

Items checked "1"—urgent attention needed—form the basis for the Customer Satisfaction Business Plan.

IX. Advertising and Sales

	No Immediate Attention Needed	Attention May Be Needed	Urgent Attention Needed
1. Do advertising messages have a positive impact on employee attitudes as well as encouraging customers to buy?	☐	☐	☐
2. Are service benefits translated into advertising messages that customers can understand and relate to?	☐	☐	☐
3. Do advertising messages feature personal service as well as material service?	☐	☐	☐
4. Are solutions for breakdowns, faults, or service failures advertised or promoted?	☐	☐	☐
5. Do advertising messages have continuity?	☐	☐	☐
6. Do advertising materials feature a consistent theme, logo, trademark, or symbol?	☐	☐	☐

	No Immediate Attention Needed	Attention May Be Needed	Urgent Attention Needed
	3	2	1
7. Are advertising messages, including direct mail efforts, seen or heard by employees?	☐	☐	☐
8. Are service guarantees meaningful to customers and used effectively?	☐	☐	☐
9. Does the projected image of all service delivery facilities support the service strategy?	☐	☐	☐
10. Does the image projected by all service delivery employees support the service strategy?	☐	☐	☐
11. Does the sales force sell service first and price second?	☐	☐	☐
12. Are service benefits sold in terms customers can understand and relate to?	☐	☐	☐
13. Can the company deliver what the selling propositions promise?	☐	☐	☐
14. Are there properly prepared sales aids for selling service?	☐	☐	☐
15. Can service advantages over competition be put across in sales propositions and advertising messages?	☐	☐	☐

Items checked "1"—urgent attention needed—form the basis for the Customer Satisfaction Business Plan.

X. Resolving Failures

1. Is the success of the company's complaint and inquiry handling units measured on the repeat business they generate?	☐	☐	☐
2. Are inquiries handled as sales opportunities or requests for assistance?	☐	☐	☐

	No Immediate Attention Needed	Attention May Be Needed	Urgent Attention Needed
	3	2	1
3. Is complainant satisfaction tracked regularly?	☐	☐	☐
4. Are the data from complaints and inquiries used at all times to conduct preventive analysis and solve problems?	☐	☐	☐
5. Are complaints and inquiries handled when first expressed rather than allowed to escalate?	☐	☐	☐
6. Is there feedback to individual employees on a regular basis from complaints and inquiries?	☐	☐	☐
7. Are complaints and inquiries used effectively for selling and cross-selling opportunities?	☐	☐	☐
8. Are customer comments, inquiries, and complaints actively solicited?	☐	☐	☐
9. Is there a regular business plan/profit plan for complaint and inquiry handling units?	☐	☐	☐
10. Are responses to complaints and inquiries handled within the time frame customers expect?	☐	☐	☐
11. Are responses to complaints and inquiries handled so that customers feel the handling has been responsive to their needs?	☐	☐	☐
12. Do all complaint and inquiry handling staff receive proper training for their jobs?	☐	☐	☐
13. Do the complaint and inquiry handling units generate a return on investment acceptable to management?	☐	☐	☐

Items checked "1"—urgent attention needed—form the basis for the Customer Satisfaction Business Plan.

	No Immediate Attention Needed	Attention May Be Needed	Urgent Attention Needed
	3	2	1

XI. Measurement and Evaluation

1. Are service delivery and customer satisfaction measured internally, through quality assurance inspections, audits, employee surveys, self-audits, etc.? ☐ ☐ ☐

2. Are service delivery and customer satisfaction evaluated, through quality circles, focus groups, management action, etc.? ☐ ☐ ☐

3. Are service delivery and customer satisfaction measured externally, through customer audits, customer satisfaction tracking systems, customer satisfaction surveys, customer comment cards, etc.? ☐ ☐ ☐

4. Are the data obtained in measurements used to produce meaningful financial data in terms of profit and revenue opportunity or market damage? ☐ ☐ ☐

5. Are this financial data on customer satisfaction reviewed, paid attention to, and actioned with the same regularity and priority as profit data? ☐ ☐ ☐

Items checked "1"—urgent attention needed—form the basis for the Customer Satisfaction Business Plan.

THE CUSTOMER SATISFACTION BUSINESS PLAN

When the Service Excellence Checklist is completed, transfer items marked "1"—urgent attention needed—to the Customer Satisfaction Business Plan. Items marked "2"—attention may be needed—should be investigated further to move them into the first or third category.

| I. | Name of company or organization: _____ |

| II. | Level of commitment |

Initial funding given: _____
Service strategy: _____
_____
_____

| III. | The right people |

Checklist item no.	Description of action needed	Person responsible for investigating	Estimated cost of action $	Estimated return on action $

| IV. | Organizational structure |

Checklist item no.	Description of action needed	Person responsible for investigating	Estimated cost of action $	Estimated return on action $

| V. | Training and development |

Checklist item no.	Description of action needed	Person responsible for investigating	Estimated cost of action $	Estimated return on action $

VI. Product/service perception				
Checklist item no.	Description of action needed	Person responsible for investigating	Estimated cost of action $	Estimated return on action $

VII. Performance				
Checklist item no.	Description of action needed	Person responsible for investigating	Estimated cost of action $	Estimated return on action $

VIII. Opportunity				
Checklist item no.	Description of action needed	Person responsible for investigating	Estimated cost of action $	Estimated return on action $

IX. Advertising and sales				
Checklist item no.	Description of action needed	Person responsible for investigating	Estimated cost of action $	Estimated return on action $

X. Resolving failures				
Checklist item no.	Description of action needed	Person responsible for investigating	Estimated cost of action $	Estimated return on action $

XI. Measurement and evaluation				
Checklist item no.	Description of action needed	Person responsible for investigating	Estimated cost of action $	Estimated return on action $

For companies truly obsessed with service excellence, this will be the first of many Customer Satisfaction Business Plans. In fact, the Customer Satisfaction Business Plan should be part of a company's overall business plan, strategic plan, and profit plan.

The journey to service excellence is not easy; the road has no end. It requires commitment and perseverance over time, but its rewards are great.

Sources

Adair, John (1983). *Effective Leadership*. London, U.K.: Gower Publishing Co. Ltd.

Albrecht, Karl and Zemke, Ron (1985). *Service America!* Homewood, IL: Dow Jones-Irwin.

Barnhart, Clarence L. (Editor in Chief 1963). *The World Book Encyclopedia Dictionary*. Chicago, IL: Doubleday & Company, Inc.

Bruce, Mike. "Managing People First—Bringing the Service Concept to British Airways." *ICT*, March/April 1987.

Cook, Harvey, R. (1969). *Selecting Advertising Media*. Washington, DC: Small Business Administration.

Crosby, Philip B. (1979). *Quality Is Free*. New York, NY: McGraw-Hill Book Company.

Davis, Richard. "How Avis Did It." *Director* magazine, London, U.K.: The Director Publications Ltd., November 1987.

Evans, Davis. "Setting Standards in Customer Care." *Marketing Week*, February 19, 1988.

Frankfort, Dawn Beth. "Milkman with the Midas Touch." *USAIR*, October 1986.

Goodman, John A. and Malech, Arlene R. (1985). "The Role of Service in Effective Marketing." *Customer Services*, New York, NY: McGraw-Hill Book Company.

Hamilton, Martha M. "In U.S., Travelers Decry Flight Delays, Overbookings, Poor Service." *International Herald Tribune*, June 15, 1987.

Kelley, Robert E. "Poorly Served Employees Serve Customers Just as Poorly." *Manager's Journal, The Wall Street Journal*, October 1987.

Koepp, Stephen. "Pul-eeze! Will Somebody Help Me?" *Time* magazine, February 2, 1987.

Leapman, Michael (1987). "Success—How Colin Marshall Makes It Work." *Expression!*, Expression Publishers.

Levering, Robert, Moskowitz, Milton, and Katz, Michael (1984). *The 100 Best Companies to Work for in America*.

Lovelock, Christopher H. (1984). *Services Marketing*. Englewood Cliffs, NJ: Prentice-Hall, Inc.

Mager, Robert F. (1962). *Preparing Instructional Objectives*. Palo Alto, California: Fearon Publishers, Inc.

McWhirter, William. "In West Germany: Picking Up a $37,142 Baby." *Time* magazine, June 22, 1987.

Morland, Julia (1987). *Quality Circles*. London, U.K.: The Industrial Society.

1981 Michelin Great Britain and Ireland. London, U.K.: Michelin Tire Co. Ltd., Tourism Department.

Olsen, Frank. "Last Word." British Airways' *Business Life* magazine. London, U.K.: Headway Publications (Number 10, August/September 1987).

Peters, Thomas J. and Waterman, Robert H. Jr. (1982). *In Search of Excellence*. New York, NY: Harper & Row.

Pierce, Kenneth M. "Like a Spiral to Heaven." *Time* magazine, June 22, 1987.

Robson, Michael (1986). *The Journey to Excellence*. New York: John Wiley & Sons, Inc.

Stone, John. "Top Executives Seek the Right Formula for 4th Quarter Success." *Business Travel News*, September 7, 1987.

Index